CONTENTS

CHAPTER 1: NINJA DT201 FOODI 10-IN-1 XL 5

CHAPTER 2: BREAKFAST 6

Bacon Toad in a Hole 6

Eggs in Purgatory 7

Asparagus Quiche...8

Raspberry Stratas 9

Bagel and Mushroom Pudding 11

Cinnamon French Toast...12

Apple Pancake...13

Chocolate Oat Bars 14

Strawberry Cocoa Popovers 15

Prosciutto Scones 16

Pecan and Blueberry Cake..17

CHAPTER 3: SNACKS AND APPETIZERS..18

Mango and Pineapple Leather 18

Creamy Kale and Bacon Ranch Dip 19

Tortilla Chips with Jalapeño Corn Dip 20

Pretzels with Beer Cheese Dip 21

Mozzarella Sausage Bread 23

Pizza Margherita..24

Spanakopita 25

Ham and Asparagus Puff Pastry Bundles..26

Artichoke and Spinach Pinwheels..27

Authentic Philly Cheese Steak Egg Rolls...28

Potato Chips with Cream Cheese Pesto Dip 29

Loaded Potato Wedges with Bacon 30

Cream Cheese Jalapeño Poppers..31

Onion Ring Fritters 32

Avocado Crab Rangoon 33

Kung Pao Chicken and Water Chestnut Totchos...34

Braised Chinese Flavor Chicken Wings..35

Beef Jerky 36

CHAPTER 4: POULTRY 37

Orange Whole Chicken with Sweet Potatoes..37

Korean Fried Whole Chicken..38

Spinach and Ham Chicken Cordon Bleu..39

Crispy Chicken Po' Boys with Coleslaw 40

Chicken Fajitas...41

Honey Chicken with Potato Wedges 42

Chicken Tacos 43

Chicken and Cannellini Bean Stew 44

Chicken Enchiladas 45

Chicken and Gouda Casserole 46

Mexican Turkey Meatloaf 47

CHAPTER 5: BEEF, PORK, AND LAMB **49**

Easy Carne Asada Tacos 49

Flank Steak with Roasted Brussels Sprouts 50

Barbecue Beef Meatloaf with Potato Cubes 51

Honey Pork with Beans and Potatoes 52

Pork Wellington 53

Cuban Pork with Fried Plantains 54

Mojito Pulled Pork Burgers 55

Chorizo and Cauliflower Rice Stuffed Peppers 56

Lamb Rack with Potato Salad 57

CHAPTER 6: SEAFOOD **58**

Cod with Potato Chips 58

Tilapia Tacos 59

Whitefish in Foil 60

Parmesan Tilapia with Asparagus 61

Mahi-Mahi with Potatoes and Pineapple 62

Salmon with Bok Choy 63

Baked Golden Shrimp 64

Butter Cracker Stuffed Shrimp 65

Chicken and Seafood Paella 66

Spicy Bacon-Stuffed Gold Clams 67

CHAPTER 7: VEGETARIAN SIDES AND MAINS **68**

Squash, Zucchini, and Eggplant Ratatouille 68

Super Cheesy Eggplant Lasagna 69

Roasted Mushroom Enchiladas 70

Coconut Tofu, Chickpea, and Kale Curry 71

Spaghetti Squash with Parmesan Mushroom 72

Classic Succotash 73

Mac and Cheese 74

Corn Bread 75

Gnocchi with Roasted Zucchini and Peppers 76

CHAPTER 8: ENTERTAINING **77**

Candied Pecans, Walnuts, and Almonds 77

Lush Snack Mix 78

Cauliflower and Asparagus Pita Platter 79

Crostini with Crab BLT Dip 80

Pull-Apart Cranberry Bread 81

Honey Ham with Orange Carrots 82

Italian Parmesan Meatball al Forno 83

Parmesan Beef Roast 84

Beef, Clam, and Veggie Hot Dish 85

Lamb Leg and Vegetable Medley 86

Quinoa and Potato Stuffed Turkey 87

Sumptuous Seafood Newburg Casserole 88

Corn Bread, Pear, and Sausage Casserole 89

Dill and Honey Butter Roasted Carrots 90

Basil Heirloom Tomato and Pepper Pie 91

Simple Roasted Baby Potatoes 92

Hearty Festival Side Dishes 93

Sweet Potato Casserole with Marshmallows 95

Creamy and Cheesy Cauliflower Gratin 96

Potato, Carrot, and Parsnip au Gratin 97

Parmesan Corn Bread 98

Apple Pies 99

CHAPTER 9: DESSERTS **100**

Pecan Cookies 100

Walnut Biscotti with Chocolate Chips 101

Chocolate and Macadamia Cookie Bars 102

Strawberry Crumble Bars 103

Lime Pie Bars 104

Chocolate Fudgy Brownies 105

Pretzel and Hazelnut Brownies 106

Ritzy Candy Bar and Cookie Cake 107

Blackberry and Raspberry Hand Pies 108

Pumpkin and Crusty Bread Pudding 109

CHAPTER 1: NINJA DT201 FOODI 10-IN-1 XL

Do you want a smart multipurpose electric oven to do all the cooking for you? Then meet the Ninja Foodi 10 in 1 XL Air fryer oven. Its large size and the multi-rack cooking system gives this smart oven an added advantage over its competitors. Ninja Foodi has launched this large-size air frying electric oven to meet the needs of people like me who love to cook at home and feed their friends and family every now and then. Now you can Air fry, roast, broil, bake, toast bread, bake a pizza and a bagel, or cook a whole roast using the smart cooking features of this amazing countertop appliance. For me, bringing the Ninja Foodi XL pro home turned out to be the smartest decision. Cooking large portion sizes in a single session was really a problem until I started using the Ninja foodi XL pro; its 4-rack cooking system not only provides enough space to accommodate large food portions inside, but the effective convection ensures that the heat passes through all the levels when needed. So, if you too want to bring this ultimate kitchen companion home, then my experience with the appliance will help big time. The collection of 500 Ninja XL pro oven recipes will let you cook a variety of meals in different sizes in a quick time. So, let's get started with some words about this oven itself.

Compared to ordinary electric and convection ovens, the convection power of the Ninja foodi XL Pro is ten times more, which leaves the air fried food extremely crispy on the outside and super moist on the inside. The best part is that you can use multiple racks to accommodate all the batches of food, which prevents overcrowding. Unlike conventional electric ovens, the Ninja Foodi XL pro has a powerful heating system that is 30 times faster than the other ovens. It was quite surprising for me as the oven preheated itself in a bare minimum of 90 seconds. So, there is no waiting around; as soon as you are done preparing the food, you can slide it into the oven right away and cook!

Besides the ten cooking operations, the user-friendly control system is the real deal. Using this oven for the very first time was just a breeze. Its prominent black control panel is present on the front-top portion, right above the glass door. There are '+' and '-'keys for each operation to change the cooking functions, the cooking temperature, and time. Then there are four layers inside the oven to adjust food. By pressing and selecting "RACK LEVEL" from 1-4, you instruct your oven to maintain the temperature at the particular level. Then the function key is used to select the cooking functions listed on the other corner of the panel: Whole roast, Air Fry, Air Crisp, Air Broil, Bake, Dehydrate, bagel, Pizza, Toast and reheat. The temperature and time keys are used to increase or decrease the values, and the same buttons are used to adjust the required darkness and number slices of the toasts and bagels functions. Once everything is set, you simply press the START/ PAUSE button to initiate preheating and then cooking.

Wasn't that quick and simple? Well, the Ninja XL pro is nothing but convenience, and you will find it to be true once you will get to cook all the delicious meals I have compiled in this cookbook, so go ahead and give them a try!

CHAPTER 2: BREAKFAST

Bacon Toad in a Hole

Prep time: 15 minutes | Cook time: 15 minutes | Serves 6

12 bacon slices

6 slices bread

3 tablespoons unsalted butter, at room temperature

Cooking oil spray

6 large eggs

½ teaspoon dried thyme

Kosher salt and freshly ground black pepper, to taste

2 tablespoons chopped fresh chives (optional)

1. Divide the bacon between the sheet pans and arrange the slices in a single layer on each.
2. Install the wire racks on Levels 1 and 3. Select BAKE, select 2 LEVEL, set the temperature to 400ºF (204ºC), and set the time to 15 minutes. Press START/STOP to begin preheating.
3. When the unit has preheated, place a sheet pan on each wire rack. Close the oven door to begin cooking.
4. Meanwhile, using a 3-inch biscuit cutter, make a hole in the center of each bread slice. Butter one side of each slice.
5. After 10 minutes of cooking, remove the sheet pans and transfer the bacon to a paper-towel-lined plate (the bacon will not be fully cooked; that's okay).
6. Leaving any rendered bacon fat on the pans, lightly coat the sheet pans with cooking spray.
7. Place the bread on the oiled sheet pans in a single layer, buttered-side down. Place 2 slices of bacon on each bread slice in an X shape, covering the hole in the bread. Crack an egg onto the center of each X, taking care not to break the yolk. Sprinkle with the thyme and season with salt and pepper.
8. Place the sheet pans in the oven and close the door to resume cooking. Bake until the egg whites have set, about 5 minutes.
9. When cooking is complete, serve immediately, garnished with the chives (if using).

Eggs in Purgatory

Prep time: 15 minutes | Cook time: 30 to 35 minutes | Serves 3 to 5

1 (15-ounce / 425-g) can tomato sauce

1 (10-ounce / 283-g) can diced tomatoes with green chiles

$^1/_3$ cup grated Parmesan cheese, divided

½ teaspoon red pepper flakes

1 teaspoon Italian seasoning

5 slices Italian or Scali bread

Extra-virgin olive oil, for drizzling

6 medium eggs

$^1/_3$ cup ricotta cheese

1 garlic clove

Kosher salt and freshly ground black pepper, to taste

Fresh basil leaves, torn, for garnish

1.	Install the wire racks on Levels 1 and 3. Select AIR ROAST, select 2 LEVEL, set the temperature to 400ºF (204ºC), and set the time to 30 minutes. Press START/STOP to begin preheating.

2.	In the pie pan, mix together the tomato sauce, diced tomatoes with green chiles, half of the Parmesan, the red pepper flakes, and Italian seasoning until combined. Place the pie pan on a sheet pan.

3.	When the unit has preheated, place the sheet pan with the tomato mixture on Level 3. Close the oven door to begin cooking. Roast for 15 minutes.

4.	Meanwhile, place the bread on the other sheet pan and drizzle with the olive oil.

5.	After the tomato mixture has roasted for 15 minutes, reduce the heat to 375ºF (191ºC). Remove the tomato mixture from the oven and stir. Make 6 wells in the mixture and crack an egg into each. Dollop the ricotta between the eggs. Insert the bread on Level 1 and close the oven door to begin cooking.

6.	After 5 minutes, flip the bread and bake another 5 minutes. Remove the bread from the oven and rub it with the garlic clove while the bread is hot. Season with salt and pepper.

7.	Return the pie pan to the oven and bake until the eggs are done to your liking—5 minutes for softer eggs, 10 minutes for well done.

8.	Garnish the dish with the remaining Parmesan and basil.

Asparagus Quiche

Prep time: 15 minutes | Cook time: 35 minutes | Serves 16

Unsalted butter, for greasing

2 frozen puff pastry sheets, thawed

10 large eggs

½ cup heavy cream

2 teaspoons kosher salt

1 teaspoon freshly ground black pepper

6 slices deli ham, cut into 1-inch strips

1½ cups shredded Cheddar cheese

5 asparagus spears, cut into ½-inch pieces

2 small yellow onions, diced

1.   Grease the pie pans with butter. Press a puff pastry sheet into the bottom and up the sides of each pie pan.

2.   Install the wire racks on Levels 1 and 3. Select BAKE, select 2 LEVEL, set the temperature to 350ºF (177ºC), and set the time to 10 minutes. Press START/STOP to begin preheating.

3.   When the unit has preheated, place a pie pan on each wire rack. Close the oven door to begin cooking.

4.   Meanwhile, in a medium bowl, whisk together the eggs, cream, salt, and pepper.

5.   After 10 minutes, remove the pans from the oven and put them on trivets or a wooden cutting board. Allow to cool for about 10 minutes.

6.   Arrange the ham and cheese in the crust of one pan and the asparagus and onions in the other. Pour the egg mixture over both, dividing equally. Select BAKE, set the temperature to 350ºF (177ºC), and set the time to 20 minutes. Press START/STOP to begin preheating.

7.   When the unit has preheated, return the pie pans to the wire racks and close the oven door to begin cooking.

8.   Cooking is complete when a toothpick in the center of the quiches comes out clean.

9.   Remove the quiches from the oven and let sit for 10 to 15 minutes. Then cut each quiche into 8 slices and serve.

Raspberry Stratas

Prep time: 20 minutes | Cook time: 1 hour | Serves 20

Cooking oil spray

1 medium sweet onion, diced

1 red bell pepper, diced

8 ounces (227 g) Canadian bacon, diced

1 tablespoon Cajun seasoning (or your favorite savory spice blend), divided

12 ounces (340 g) day-old crusty bread, cut into 1-inch cubes (about 4 packed cups), divided

2 cups shredded Cheddar cheese

16 large eggs, divided

4 cups whole milk, divided

1 cup heavy cream, divided

Kosher salt, to taste, plus ¼ teaspoon

Freshly ground black pepper, to taste

14 ounces (397 g) day-old brioche bread, cut into 1-inch cubes (about 4 packed cups), divided

2 tablespoons vanilla extract, divided

Grated zest of 1 lemon

2 cups ricotta cheese, divided

1 (12-ounce / 340-g) jar raspberry preserves, divided

$^1/_3$ cup sliced almonds

1.   Lightly coat the casserole dishes with cooking spray.

2.   In a large skillet over high heat, combine the onion, bell pepper, Canadian bacon, and ½ tablespoon of Cajun seasoning. Sauté until the onion is golden and fragrant and the bacon lightly browned, about 5 minutes.

3.   To assemble the savory strata: Place half the crusty bread cubes in one of the prepared casserole dishes. Top with three-quarters of the cooked bacon-and-onion mixture and 1 cup of Cheddar. Top with the remaining crusty bread cubes and the cooked bacon-and-onion mixture.

4.   In a large bowl, whisk together 8 eggs, 2 cups of milk, ½ cup of cream, and the remaining ½ tablespoon of Cajun seasoning, and season with salt and pepper. Slowly pour the egg mixture into the casserole dish. Push the bread down into the liquid, adding more milk if necessary, so the bread is just barely submerged when pressed down.

5.   To assemble the sweet strata: Place half the brioche cubes in the other casserole dish. In another large bowl (or wash and dry the used bowl), whisk together the remaining 8 eggs, remaining 2 cups of milk, remaining ½ cup of cream, the vanilla, lemon zest, and ¼ teaspoon of salt. Pour half the mixture over the brioche cubes in the dish.

6.   Dollop 1½ cups of ricotta by the spoonful over the top, followed by three-quarters of the preserves. Use a spatula to spread the ricotta and preserves over the entire surface area of the layer of bread, then sprinkle the almonds on top.

7.   Arrange the remaining brioche cubes on top, then pour the remaining egg mixture over them. Spoon the remaining ½ cup of ricotta over the strata, followed by the remaining preserves.

8.   Cover both stratas with foil and refrigerate for at least 6 hours or overnight.

9.   After the stratas have been chilled, install the wire racks on Levels 1 and 3. Select BAKE, select 2 LEVEL, set the temperature to 350ºF (177ºC), and set the time to 60 minutes. Press START/STOP to begin preheating.

10.   When the unit has preheated, place a covered casserole dish on each wire rack. Close the oven door to begin cooking.

11.   When there are 20 minutes remaining, carefully remove the foil from both stratas, and top the savory strata with the remaining 1 cup of Cheddar cheese. Continue cooking, uncovered.

12.   Cooking is complete when the stratas are golden brown on top and a knife inserted into the center comes out clean. Let cool for 5 minutes before serving.

Bagel and Mushroom Pudding

Prep time: 15 minutes | Cook time: 40 minutes | Serves 8

2 (8-ounce / 227-g) containers white button mushrooms, stemmed and halved

2 tablespoons canola oil

Kosher salt and freshly ground black pepper, to taste

6 large eggs

2 cups heavy cream

1 (6-ounce / 170-g) bag shredded Swiss cheese

6 plain bagels, cut or torn into cubes

1.   In a large bowl, combine the mushrooms and oil, and season with salt and pepper. Mix well to combine. Place the mushrooms in the air fryer basket.

2.   Ensure no wire racks are in the oven. Select AIR FRY, set the temperature to 390ºF (199ºC), and set the time to 10 minutes. Press START/STOP to begin preheating.

3.   When the unit has preheated, insert the air fryer basket on Level 3. Close the oven door to begin cooking.

4.   In another large bowl (or wash and dry the used bowl), whisk together the eggs and cream, and season with salt and pepper. Add the cheese and mix again.

5.   When the mushrooms have completed cooking, remove the basket from the oven. Let cool for about 5 minutes, then add the mushrooms to the egg mixture. Add the bagel pieces and, using your hands, mix well to combine. Pour the mixture into the casserole dish and press down gently to make the mixture sit flat.

6.   If necessary, remove the crumb tray from the oven and wash away any mushroom bits. Install the wire rack on Level 3. Select BAKE, set the temperature to 350ºF (177ºC), and set the time to 30 minutes. Press START/STOP to begin preheating.

7.   When the unit has preheated, place the casserole on the wire rack. Close the oven door to begin cooking.

8.   When cooking is complete, remove from the oven and let cool for 5 minutes before serving.

Cinnamon French Toast

Prep time: 20 minutes | Cook time: 45 to 55 minutes | Serves 6 to 10

Cooking oil spray

For the French toast base

1 (8-ounce / 227-g) package cream cheese, at room temperature

2 tablespoons powdered sugar

Grated zest and juice of 1 lemon

6 large eggs, beaten

1 cup whole milk

$^1/_3$ cup packed light brown sugar

2 teaspoons vanilla extract

½ teaspoon ground cinnamon

18 (1-ounce / 28-g) Hawaiian sweet rolls, quartered

For the topping

½ cup all-purpose flour

$^1/_3$ cup packed light brown sugar

½ teaspoon ground cinnamon

4 tablespoons (½ stick) cold unsalted butter, cut into 3 pieces

1.   Coat the baking pan with cooking spray and set aside.

2.   To make the French toast base: Using a hand mixer or stand mixer, beat together the cream cheese, powdered sugar, and lemon zest and juice until creamy.

3.   In a large bowl, mix together the eggs, milk, brown sugar, vanilla, and cinnamon until well combined. Fold the rolls into the egg mixture, swirl the cream cheese mixture in, then pour into the prepared pan.

4.   To make the topping: In a small bowl, mix together the flour, brown sugar, and cinnamon. Using your fingers, work the cold butter into the dry ingredients. The topping should look like small pebbles. Sprinkle the topping evenly over the French toast base.

5.   Install a wire rack on Level 3. Select BAKE, set the temperature to 350ºF (177ºC), and set the time to 45 minutes. Press START/STOP to begin preheating.

6.   When the unit has preheated, place the sheet pan on the wire rack. Close the oven door to begin cooking.

7.   Bake for 30 minutes for a softer texture or up to 55 minutes for a firmer, crispier texture.

Apple Pancake

Prep time: 10 minutes | Cook time: 15 minutes | Serves 8 to 12

Cooking oil spray

For the Pancake:

4 cups pancake mix

2 tablespoons apple pie spice

2 cups milk

4 large eggs

¼ cup applesauce

2 teaspoons vanilla extract

1 apple, cored, peeled, and thinly sliced

For the Glaze:

1 cup powdered sugar

1 teaspoon apple pie spice

2 tablespoons apple juice

¼ cup pecans, chopped

1. Coat the sheet pan with cooking spray and set aside.
2. To make the pancake: In a large bowl, whisk together the pancake mix, apple pie spice, milk, eggs, applesauce, and vanilla until well combined.
3. Install a wire rack on Level 3. Select BAKE, set the temperature to 425ºF (218ºC), and set the time to 15 minutes. Press START/STOP to begin preheating.
4. Pour the batter onto the prepared sheet pan and use a spatula to spread it into an even layer. Arrange the apple slices evenly on top of the batter.
5. When the unit has preheated, place the sheet pan on the wire rack. Close the oven door to begin cooking.
6. To make the glaze: In a small bowl, whisk together the powdered sugar, apple pie spice, and apple juice until smooth and pourable.
7. The pancake is finished cooking when a toothpick inserted in the center comes out clean. Remove the pan from the oven and cut the pancake into your desired dimensions. Drizzle it with the glaze and sprinkle with the pecans.

Chocolate Oat Bars

Prep time: 10 minutes | Cook time: 20 minutes | Makes 12 to 14 bars

1 cup maple almond butter

¼ cup packed light brown sugar

¼ cup honey

2 large eggs

2 teaspoons vanilla extract

2 cups old-fashioned rolled oats

1 cup whole-wheat flour

1 teaspoon baking soda

1 cup semisweet chocolate chips

1.　　In a large bowl, mix together the almond butter, brown sugar, honey, eggs, and vanilla until fully combined.

2.　　In a separate large bowl, mix together the oats, flour, and baking soda. Fold the flour mixture into the egg mixture until fully combined. Add the chocolate chips and mix to combine.

3.　　Line the sheet pan with parchment paper. Spread the batter onto the pan and spread evenly with a spatula or knife.

4.　　Install a wire rack on Level 3. Select BAKE, set the temperature to 325ºF (163ºC), and set the time to 20 minutes. Press START/STOP to begin preheating.

5.　　When the unit has preheated, place the sheet pan on the wire rack. Close the oven door to begin cooking.

6.　　Cooking is complete when the top is set and golden brown in color. Remove the pan from the oven and let cool completely in the pan, then cut into bars before serving.

Strawberry Cocoa Popovers

Prep time: 5 minutes | Cook time: 11 minutes | Makes 12 popovers

For the Popovers:

¾ cup all-purpose flour

¾ cup whole milk, warmed

3 large eggs

1 packet instant hot cocoa

1 tablespoon sugar

1 tablespoon ground cinnamon

½ teaspoon salt

1 teaspoon vanilla

2 tablespoons cold unsalted butter, cut into 12 small cubes

For the Topping:

2 tablespoons unsalted butter, at room temperature

2 tablespoons strawberry jam

1 packet instant hot cocoa

Powdered sugar, for sprinkling

1. To make the popovers: Put the flour, milk, eggs, hot cocoa, sugar, cinnamon, salt, and vanilla in a blender and pulse until the batter is smooth.

2. Place 1 cube of butter into each muffin tin well. Install a wire rack on Level 3, place the muffin tin on the rack, and close the oven door. Select BAKE, set the temperature to 425ºF (218ºC), and set the time to 11 minutes. Press START/STOP to begin preheating.

3. When the unit has preheated, carefully remove the hot muffin tin. Pour the batter evenly into the cups on top of the melted butter so the cups are about three-quarters full.

4. Return the muffin tin to the wire rack. Close the oven door to begin cooking.

5. Bake for 10 minutes, until the tops are brown. Do not open the oven door during cooking.

6. To make the topping: While the popovers are baking, combine the butter, jam, and hot cocoa in a small bowl. Set aside.

7. When 1 minute of cooking remains, remove the muffin tin from the oven and distribute the chocolate topping evenly among the popovers. Continue cooking for 1 minute, or until the topping is softened.

8. Serve warm sprinkled with powdered sugar.

Prosciutto Scones

Prep time: 10 minutes | Cook time: 23 to 27 minutes | Serves 8 to 12

6 thin slices prosciutto

1½ cups pancake and baking mix

8 tablespoons (1 stick) cold unsalted butter, cut into small pieces

¼ cup whole milk, plus more if needed

2 tablespoons freeze-dried or fresh chives

½ cup shredded Parmesan cheese

1 tablespoon unsalted butter, melted

1.   Lay the prosciutto slices flat on the sheet pan.

2.   Install a wire rack on Level 3. Select BAKE, set the temperature to 400ºF (204ºC), and set the time to 10 minutes. Press START/STOP to begin preheating.

3.   When the unit has preheated, place the sheet pan on the wire rack. Close the oven door to begin cooking.

4.   When the prosciutto is cooked and crispy, transfer it to paper towels to drain. Pour off any fat from the sheet pan and wipe it dry.

5.   Pour the pancake mix into a large bowl. Add the cold butter and, using a pastry cutter or two knives, cut it into the mix until the butter is in small pieces no larger than peas.

6.   Make a well in the center, pour in the milk, and add the chives. Gently stir together with a wooden spoon until well incorporated. The dough should be slightly sticky. If the mixture seems too dry, add an additional tablespoon of milk.

7.   Roughly chop the cooked prosciutto into small pieces and add to the dough along with the Parmesan. Stir well to combine.

8.   Shape the dough into a large circle about ½ inch thick and place it on the sheet pan. Using a sharp knife, cut the dough into 8 wedges. Brush the top of the dough with the melted butter.

9.   Select BAKE, set the temperature to 400ºF (204ºC), and set the time to 20 minutes. Press START/STOP to begin preheating.

10.   When the unit has preheated, place the sheet pan on the wire rack. Close the oven door to begin cooking.

11.   Check the scones after 13 to 17 minutes. They are finished cooking when they are lightly golden brown and firm to the touch. Remove the pan from the oven. Let cool before dividing into individual scones.

Pecan and Blueberry Cake

Prep time: 20 minutes | Cook time: 1 hour | Serves 10

Cooking oil spray

8 tablespoons (1 stick) unsalted butter, at room temperature

1 cup packed dark brown sugar

1 cup all-purpose flour

¾ cup chopped pecans

1 teaspoon ground cinnamon

½ teaspoon kosher salt

1 (16-ounce / 454-g) box yellow cake mix

1 (3.4-ounce / 96-g) packet lemon instant pudding

3 large eggs

½ cup canola oil

1 cup water

2 cups fresh blueberries, divided

1.   Coat the casserole dish with the cooking spray and set aside.

2.   In a small bowl, mix the butter, brown sugar, flour, pecans, cinnamon, and salt until combined. Set the streusel aside.

3.   In a large bowl, mix the cake mix, pudding, eggs, oil, and water until smooth. Pour half the batter into the prepared casserole dish.

4.   Top with 1½ cups of blueberries. Pour the remaining batter over the blueberries, then top with the remaining ½ cup of blueberries and the streusel.

5.   Install a wire rack on Level 2. Select BAKE, set the temperature to 350ºF (177ºC), and set the time to 60 minutes. Press START/STOP to begin preheating.

6.   When the unit has preheated, place the casserole dish on the wire rack. Close the oven door to begin cooking.

7.   The cake is done when a toothpick inserted in the center comes out clean.

CHAPTER 3: SNACKS AND APPETIZERS

Mango and Pineapple Leather

Prep time: 10 minutes | Cook time: 6 to 8 minutes | Makes 15 leather strips

2 cups cubed mango

2 cups cubed pineapple

2 tablespoons honey

1.   Put the mango and pineapple in a blender. Blend until smooth. Add the honey a little bit at a time, to taste.

2.   Line the sheet pan with parchment paper (do not use wax paper).

3.   Using a spatula, spread the fruit mixture over the parchment paper in an even layer, making it as thin as possible.

4.   Install the wire rack on Level 3. Select DEHYDRATE, set the temperature to 150ºF (66ºC), and set the time for 8 hours. Press START/STOP to begin preheating.

5.   When the unit has preheated, place the sheet pan on the wire rack. Close the oven door to begin dehydrating.

6.   Check the fruit leather after 6 hours. It is done when it is dry and firm all the way through. Gently touch the leather in the center, and if the pressure creates an indent, it's not finished. If more time is needed, dehydrate for up to 2 hours more.

7.   Remove the pan from the oven and let cool completely before cutting.

Creamy Kale and Bacon Ranch Dip

Prep time: 15 minutes | Cook time: 1 hour | Serves 6 to 8

8 thick-cut bacon slices

1 (10-ounce / 283-g) package frozen chopped kale, thawed and squeezed dry

1 (8-ounce / 227-g) package cream cheese, at room temperature

1 (1-ounce / 28-g) packet ranch dressing mix

1 cup sour cream

$^1/_3$ cup sliced scallions, divided

¼ cup mayonnaise

1 cup shredded Swiss cheese blend, divided

½ teaspoon red pepper flakes

Kosher salt and freshly ground black pepper, to taste

1. Lay the bacon in the air fryer basket in a single layer.
2. Install a wire rack on Level 2. Select AIR FRY, set the temperature to 400ºF (204ºC), and set the time to 20 minutes. Press START/STOP to begin preheating.
3. When the unit has preheated, place the sheet pan on the wire rack to catch any drippings, and insert the air fryer basket on Level 3. Close the oven door to begin cooking.
4. Cook the bacon 15 to 20 minutes, flipping every 5 minutes, or until cooked to your liking. Transfer the bacon to a paper-towel-lined plate to drain, and remove the sheet pan. Once the bacon is cool, chop it.
5. In a large bowl, combine half of the bacon, the kale, cream cheese, ranch dressing mix, sour cream, half of the scallions, the mayonnaise, ½ cup of Swiss cheese blend, and the red pepper flakes until well mixed. Season with salt and pepper.
6. Spoon the mixture into the baking pan, spreading it evenly over the bottom.
7. Select BAKE, set the temperature to 375ºF (191ºC), and set the time to 20 minutes. Raise the wire rack to the Level 3 position. Press START/STOP to begin preheating.
8. Once the unit has preheated, place the baking pan on the wire rack. Close the oven door to begin cooking.
9. When cooking is complete, the dip will be bubbling around the edges. Remove the pan from the oven and top the dip with the remaining ½ cup of Swiss cheese blend.
10. Select BROIL, set the temperature to HI, and set the time to 4 minutes. Press START/STOP to begin.
11. Place the sheet pan on the wire rack and close the oven door to begin cooking. Broil for 2 to 4 minutes, or until the top is golden brown.
12. Remove the dip from the oven and top it with the remaining scallions and the bacon. Serve warm.

Tortilla Chips with Jalapeño Corn Dip

Prep time: 20 minutes | Cook time: 20 minutes | Serves 8

2 tablespoons canola oil, divided

1 (12-ounce / 340-g) bag frozen corn

1 medium red onion, diced

2 jalapeños, finely diced

1 red bell pepper, diced

1 (4.5-ounce / 128-g) can green chiles, drained

2 cups shredded pepper Jack cheese, divided

1 cup grated Parmesan cheese

½ cup mayonnaise

Kosher salt, to taste

15 (6-inch) flour tortillas

1.   In a large skillet over high heat, heat 1 tablespoon of oil. Once hot, add the corn, onion, jalapeños, and bell pepper and sauté for 5 minutes, then remove from heat.

2.   Add the green chiles, 1 cup of pepper Jack, the Parmesan, and mayonnaise. Mix well. Transfer the mixture to a casserole dish and top with the remaining pepper Jack cheese.

3.   Install a wire rack on Level 1. Select AIR FRY, select 2 LEVEL, set the temperature to 405ºF (207ºC), and set the time to 20 minutes. Press START/STOP to begin preheating.

4.   When the unit has preheated, place the casserole dish on the wire rack. Close the oven door to begin cooking

5.   Meanwhile, cut the tortillas into quarters and place in an even layer in the air fryer basket. Brush the tortillas with the remaining 1 tablespoon of canola oil and sprinkle with salt.

6.   After 5 minutes, open the door and insert the air fryer basket on Level 3.

7.   When cooking is complete, remove the bubbling dip and crispy chips from the oven. Serve warm.

Pretzels with Beer Cheese Dip

Prep time: 10 minutes | Cook time: 20 minutes | Serves 8 to 16

For the Pretzels:

1½ cups warm water

1 tablespoon sugar

1 packet (2¼ teaspoons) active dry yeast

4½ cups all-purpose flour, plus more for dusting

1 tablespoon kosher salt

3 tablespoons vegetable oil, divided

$^2/_3$ cup baking soda

2 large eggs, beaten with a splash of water

1 tablespoon unsalted butter, melted

Coarse salt, to taste

For the Beer Cheese Dip:

2 tablespoons unsalted butter

2 tablespoons all-purpose flour

1 cup lager-style beer

½ cup whole milk

1½ teaspoons Dijon mustard

1 teaspoon Worcestershire sauce

½ teaspoon smoked paprika

1 cup shredded Cheddar cheese

1 cup shredded pepper Jack cheese

Kosher salt and freshly ground black pepper, to taste

¼ cup sliced scallions

1.   To make the pretzels: In a large bowl, mix the water and sugar until combined. Stir in the yeast and set aside to rest for 5 minutes, until the yeast starts to foam.

2.   Add the flour, salt, and 2 tablespoons of oil. Mix thoroughly until a dough forms.

3.   Remove the dough from the bowl and use the remaining 1 tablespoon of oil to grease the inside of the bowl. Place the dough back in the bowl and cover with plastic wrap. Leave in a warm place for 1 hour. The dough should double in size.

4.   Once the dough has risen, fill a large pot of water about half full and heat over high heat. Whisk in the baking soda and bring to a rolling boil.

5.   While the water comes to a boil, dust a clean work surface with some flour. Turn the dough out onto the surface and cut it into 16 pieces. Roll each piece into medium-thin ropes and shape them into sticks.

6.   Once the water is boiling, add the pretzel sticks, 3 or 4 at a time, and boil on one side for 30 seconds. Flip over each stick and boil for 30 seconds more. Transfer them to a sheet pan. Repeat with the remaining pretzel sticks, distributing them evenly between the two sheet pans.

7.   Brush the tops of the pretzel sticks with the egg wash.

8.   Install the wire racks on Levels 1 and 3. Select BAKE, select 2 LEVEL, set the temperature to 450ºF (232ºC), and set the time to 15 minutes. Press START/STOP to begin preheating.

9.   When the unit has preheated, place a sheet pan on each wire rack. Close the oven door to begin cooking.

10.   Bake the pretzels for 10 to 15 minutes, until golden brown.

11.   Remove the pans from the oven. Brush the pretzel sticks with the melted butter and sprinkle with coarse salt.

12.   To make the beer cheese dip: Melt the butter in a large saucepan or sauté pan over medium-high heat. Once melted, add the flour and whisk until completely combined. Add the beer, milk, mustard, Worcestershire sauce, and paprika, and whisk until smooth. Continue cooking until the mixture has thickened and has nearly reached a simmer.

13.   Add the cheeses and whisk until smooth. Season with salt and pepper. Reduce the heat to low and cook for 2 minutes. Remove the pan from the heat. Transfer the dip to a heatproof bowl, top with the scallions, and serve alongside the pretzels.

Mozzarella Sausage Bread

Prep time: 15 minutes | Cook time: 35 minutes | Serves 8 to 12

1 (1-pound / 454-g) premium pork sausage roll

1 medium onion, chopped

1 tablespoon minced garlic

2 tablespoons dried sage

Kosher salt and freshly ground black pepper, to taste

All-purpose flour, for dusting

1 (1-pound / 454-g) package store-bought pizza dough, at room temperature

4 cups shredded Mozzarella cheese, divided

1 large egg, beaten

Marinara sauce, for dipping

1.   In a large bowl, using your hands or a whisk, break the sausage into very small chunks. Add the onion and garlic and mix well. Spread the mixture evenly on a sheet pan.

2.   Install a wire rack on Level 3. Select AIR FRY, set the temperature to 350ºF (177ºC), and set the time to 15 minutes. Press START/STOP to begin preheating.

3.   When the unit has preheated, place the sheet pan on the wire rack. Close the oven door to begin cooking.

4.   When cooking is complete, drain off any oil. Transfer the sausage to a medium bowl. Add the sage, season with salt and pepper, and toss to combine.

5.   Dust a clean work surface and rolling pin with flour. Place the pizza dough on the surface and roll it out into a rectangle no longer than the length of the sheet pan. Try not to let it get any thin spots or holes.

6.   Sprinkle 2 cups of Mozzarella evenly over the dough, leaving a 1-inch border. Using a slotted spoon, evenly spread the sausage mixture over the cheese. Sprinkle the remaining 2 cups of Mozzarella over the sausage.

7.   Starting at one of the longer sides, roll up the dough like a log, but tuck in the ends like a burrito just before you get to the end of the roll. Place the log seam-side down on the other sheet pan and brush with the beaten egg.

8.   Select BAKE, set the temperature to 350ºF (177ºC), and set the time to 35 minutes. Press START/STOP to begin preheating.

9.   When the unit has preheated, place the sheet pan on the wire rack and close the oven door to begin cooking.

10.   Bake until golden brown, adding up to 5 more minutes at the end if needed.

11.   Let the bread rest for 10 minutes. Slice and serve with marinara sauce.

Pizza Margherita

Prep time: 20 minutes | Cook time: 15 minutes | Makes 12 to 16 slices

28 ounces (794 g) store-bought pizza dough, at room temperature
All-purpose flour, for dusting
1 cup marinara sauce, divided
2 (5-ounce / 142-g) balls fresh Mozzarella cheese, cut into ½-inch slices, divided
1 bunch fresh basil, torn

1. Divide the pizza dough into two balls. Lightly flour a large, clean work surface and place one of the dough balls on it and dust the top with flour. Press around the dough by pinching with your fingers to form the edges of the crust. Starting from the center of the dough, use a flour-dusted rolling pin or your hands to push the dough outward to stretch it into a rectangle shape. Flip the dough over and repeat. Lightly flour the dough as needed to retain its stretched shape.
2. Lightly flour the sheet pan. Transfer the dough to the pan and continue stretching it out by hand to cover the pan, about 11 by 13 inches. Do not worry about it fitting perfectly.
3. Install the wire rack on Level 2. Select PIZZA, set the temperature to 450ºF (232ºC), and set the time to 10 minutes. Press START/STOP to begin preheating.
4. When the unit has preheated, place the sheet pan on the wire rack. Close the door to begin cooking.
5. After 10 minutes, remove the pan with the partially cooked dough and allow it to cool enough to handle.
6. Remove the crust from the pan and place it on a large cutting board or clean work surface. Spread ½ cup of marinara sauce over the crust. Cover with half of the sliced Mozzarella cheese.
7. Select PIZZA again, set the temperature to 450ºF (232ºC), and set the time to 15 minutes. Press START/STOP to begin preheating.
8. When the unit has preheated, using a spatula or pizza peel, slide the pizza directly onto the wire rack. Close the oven door to begin cooking.
9. After 10 minutes, check the pizza for doneness. If you prefer a crispier crust, cook for up to 5 more minutes.
10. While the pizza is cooking, repeat steps 1 and 2 for the second pizza, or place the dough in a resealable bag and refrigerate it, the remaining marinara, and remaining Mozzarella for later use.
11. Carefully remove the pizza from the oven and let cool for 5 minutes. If cooking the second pizza right away, proceed from step 3. Evenly arrange the basil on the pizza before slicing and serving.

Spanakopita

Prep time: 20 minutes | Cook time: 20 minutes | Serves 8

2 (10-ounce / 283-g) packages frozen spinach, thawed
½ tablespoon canola oil
1 medium yellow onion, diced
2 garlic cloves, minced
6 ounces (170 g) feta cheese, crumbled
Grated zest of 1 lemon
Kosher salt and freshly ground black pepper, to taste
2 frozen puff pastry sheets, thawed in refrigerator for 6 hours
1 cup all-purpose flour
1 large egg, beaten

1.   Place the thawed spinach in a clean dish towel and squeeze over the sink to remove as much moisture as possible. Chop and place in a medium bowl.
2.   In a medium skillet over medium-high heat, heat the oil. Once it is hot, add the onion and garlic and sauté until fragrant and translucent, about 5 minutes.
3.   Add the onion mixture, feta, and lemon zest to the spinach. Season with salt and pepper. Mix until thoroughly combined.
4.   Have a round object about 11 inches in diameter, like a lid to a stockpot or a mixing bowl, on hand. Place 1 sheet of puff pastry on parchment paper. Dust some of the flour on both sides of the dough. Using a flour-dusted rolling pin, roll out the dough on all sides until it will fit on a sheet pan with a 1- to 2-inch border around the edges.
5.   Place the round object in the center of the dough and press down. Remove the object and cut out the excess dough around the circle, using the imprint as your guide.
6.   Place the dough circle in the refrigerator on the parchment while you repeat steps 4 and 5 with the second sheet of puff pastry.
7.   Using a pastry brush, brush some of the egg over the second dough circle. Spread the spinach mixture in an even layer over the dough, leaving a 1-inch border. Place the chilled dough circle on top and press the edges of the two circles together to seal.
8.   Press a small cup (about 2 inches in diameter) in the center of the dough to make an indent. Chill in the refrigerator for about 10 minutes.
9.   Using a chef's knife, cut the dough into quarters starting from the edge of the small circular indent in the center. Then cut those 4 quarters in half the same way, creating 8 sections. Finally, cut those 8 sections in half, for a total of 16 sections.
10.   Using the parchment paper to help lift it, transfer the pastry to the sheet pan, trimming the edges of paper to fit if necessary. Twist each of the 16 sections three times by gently pulling to elongate each section and twisting it clockwise. Return to the refrigerator to chill for 10 more minutes.
11.   Brush the remaining egg over the top of the pastry and, if desired, sprinkle the top with salt and pepper.
12.   Install a wire rack on Level 2. Select BAKE, set the temperature to 375ºF (191ºC), and set the time to 30 minutes. Press START/STOP to begin preheating.
13.   When the unit has preheated, place the sheet pan on the wire rack. Close the oven door to begin cooking.
14.   The spanakopita is done when it has risen and the top is crispy and brown. Cook for up to 5 minutes more if needed.

Ham and Asparagus Puff Pastry Bundles

Prep time: 15 minutes | Cook time: 15 to 20 minutes | Serves 12

Cooking oil spray

All-purpose flour, for dusting

2 frozen puff pastry sheets, thawed in refrigerator

1 bunch asparagus, woody ends trimmed

1 tablespoon extra-virgin olive oil

½ teaspoon kosher salt

½ teaspoon freshly ground black pepper

6 slices deli ham, halved

6 slices Swiss cheese, halved

1 large egg, beaten

1.   Coat the sheet pans with cooking spray and set aside.

2.   On a lightly floured work surface, use a flour-dusted rolling pin to roll out each puff pastry sheet to about double its original size. Using a sharp knife, cut each sheet into 6 squares.

3.   In a large bowl, toss the asparagus in the olive oil and season with salt and pepper.

4.   On top of each puff pastry square, place a half slice of ham and a half slice of cheese. Divide the asparagus spears evenly among the squares and lay them diagonally over the cheese. Lift two opposite corners of each pastry square and wrap them around the asparagus. Press to seal.

5.   Brush the bundles with the egg. Sprinkle with more salt and pepper if desired. Place them evenly spaced on the prepared sheet pans.

6.   Install the wire racks on Levels 1 and 3. Select BAKE, select 2 LEVEL, set the temperature to 425ºF (218ºC), and set the time to 20 minutes. Press START/STOP to begin preheating.

7.   When the unit has preheated, place a sheet pan on each wire rack. Close the oven door to begin cooking.

8.   Bake for 15 to 20 minutes, or until the puff pastry is golden brown.

Artichoke and Spinach Pinwheels

Prep time: 20 minutes | Cook time: 15 minutes | Makes 16 pinwheels

1 (14-ounce / 397-g) can artichoke hearts, drained and chopped

2 cups baby spinach, chopped

½ cup sour cream

1 (8-ounce / 227-g) package cream cheese

$^1/_3$ cup mayonnaise

1 garlic clove

¼ teaspoon onion powder

Kosher salt and freshly ground black pepper, to taste

1 cup shredded Mozzarella cheese

¼ cup grated Parmesan cheese

2 (8-ounce / 227-g) tubes crescent rolls

Cooking oil spray

1 large egg, beaten

1.   In a large bowl, combine the artichoke hearts, spinach, sour cream, cream cheese, mayonnaise, garlic, and onion powder. Season with salt and pepper. Add the Mozzarella and Parmesan cheeses and stir to combine.

2.   Unroll 1 tube of crescent rolls and press the perforations to seal, creating a rectangle about 13 by 18 inches. Repeat with second tube of crescent rolls.

3.   Divide the spinach-artichoke mixture between the two rectangles, spreading it into an even layer across the surface of each.

4.   Starting at the shortest side, roll up each rectangle to create a log, and press the visible edges to seal. Cut each log crosswise into 8 pieces.

5.   Lightly coat the two sheet pans with cooking spray. Arrange the pinwheels cut-side down on the two pans. Brush the tops of the pinwheels with the egg.

6.   Install the wire racks on Levels 1 and 3. Select AIR ROAST, select 2 LEVEL, set the temperature to 375ºF (191ºC), and set the time to 15 minutes. Press START/STOP to begin preheating.

7.   When the unit has preheated, place the sheet pans on the wire racks. Close the oven door to begin cooking.

8.   When cooking is complete, let the pinwheels cool slightly before serving.

Authentic Philly Cheese Steak Egg Rolls

Prep time: 15 minutes | Cook time: 15 minutes | Makes 12 egg rolls

1 pound (454 g) finely ground beef

1 green bell pepper, chopped

1 white onion, chopped

1 tablespoon Worcestershire sauce

Kosher salt and freshly ground black pepper, to taste

12 square egg roll wrappers

6 slices American cheese, halved

Cooking oil spray

1.   In a large bowl, combine the ground beef, bell pepper, onion, and Worcestershire sauce. Season with salt and pepper.

2.   Lay out an egg roll wrapper and place a half slice of cheese in the center. Spoon 2 to 3 tablespoons of filling over the cheese slice. Fold in the sides of the wrapper and roll it up around the filling, using water to seal the edge. Coat the egg roll on all sides with cooking spray. Repeat with the remaining wrappers, cheese, and filling.

3.   Evenly arrange the egg rolls in the air fryer basket.

4.   Select AIR FRY, set the temperature to 400ºF (204ºC), and set the time to 15 minutes. Press START/STOP to begin preheating.

5.   When the unit has preheated, insert the air fryer basket on Level 3. Close the oven door to begin cooking.

6.   When cooking is complete, let the egg rolls cool before serving.

Potato Chips with Cream Cheese Pesto Dip

Prep time: 10 minutes | Cook time: 30 minutes | Serves 4 to 6

1 pound (454 g) russet potatoes, peeled

12 ounces (340 g) cream cheese, at room temperature

1 (9-ounce / 255-g) jar pesto

¼ cup grated Parmesan cheese

¼ cup vegetable oil

Kosher salt, to taste

1. Using a mandoline or a sharp knife, cut the potatoes into ⅛-inch-thick slices. Place the slices in a large bowl and cover them with cool water. Let soak for 30 minutes.

2. Spread the cream cheese in the bottom of a small oven-safe bowl. Cover with the pesto and sprinkle with the Parmesan.

3. Remove the potatoes from the water and dry them well on a clean kitchen towel. Coat the slices with the oil and arrange them in the air fryer basket in a single, even layer.

4. Install a wire rack on Level 2. Select AIR FRY, select 2 LEVEL, set the temperature to 425ºF (218ºC), and set the time to 30 minutes. Press START/STOP to begin preheating

5. When the oven has preheated, insert the air fryer basket on Level 4, and place the bowl on the wire rack. Close the oven door to begin cooking.

6. When cooking is complete, season the crisps with salt. Serve warm with the dip.

Loaded Potato Wedges with Bacon

Prep time: 10 minutes | Cook time: 25 minutes | Serves 8 to 12

2 pounds (907 g) russet potatoes, cut into wedges

2 tablespoons extra-virgin olive oil

1 tablespoon garlic powder

1 tablespoon onion powder

1 tablespoon paprika

2 teaspoons kosher salt

2 teaspoons freshly ground black pepper

8 bacon slices

2 cups shredded Cheddar cheese

½ cup sour cream

1 bunch fresh chives or scallions, thinly sliced

1.   Place the potato wedges in a large bowl. Drizzle them with the olive oil and sprinkle with the garlic powder, onion powder, paprika, salt, and pepper. Toss to evenly coat.

2.   Arrange the wedges in the air fryer basket evenly in a single layer and set aside.

3.   Lay the bacon in an even layer on the roast tray set into a sheet pan.

4.   Install a wire rack on Level 2. Select AIR FRY, select 2 LEVEL, set the temperature to 400ºF (204ºC), and set the time to 20 minutes. Press START/STOP to begin preheating.

5.   When the unit has preheated, place the roast tray and sheet pan on the wire rack and insert the air fryer basket on Level 4. Close the oven door to begin cooking

6.   After 10 minutes, remove the bacon from the oven. Let the bacon cool, then crumble it.

7.   After another 10 minutes, check the potatoes. They should be fork-tender and golden brown. Remove the basket from the oven and evenly top the potato wedges with the cheese.

8.   Select BROIL, set the temperature to HI, and set the time to 5 minutes. Press START/STOP to begin.

9.   Place the basket on the sheet pan, and place both on the wire rack. Close the oven door to begin cooking.

10.   When cooking is complete, remove the basket from the oven. Transfer the potatoes to a platter and top them with the sour cream, bacon, and chives before serving.

Cream Cheese Jalapeño Poppers

Prep time: 20 minutes | Cook time: 15 minutes | Serves 6 to 8

12 ounces (340 g) cream cheese, at room temperature

½ cup grated Parmesan cheese

2 teaspoons garlic powder

2 teaspoons smoked paprika

1 teaspoon kosher salt

1 teaspoon freshly ground black pepper

¼ cup bacon bits

12 jalapeño peppers, halved lengthwise and seeded

1.   In a medium bowl, mix together the cream cheese, Parmesan cheese, garlic power, paprika, salt, black pepper, and bacon bits until well combined.

2.   Stuff the jalapeño halves with the cream cheese mixture. Place the stuffed jalapeños in the air fryer basket in a single layer.

3.   Install a wire rack on Level 1. Select AIR FRY, set the temperature to 425ºF (218ºC), and set the time to 15 minutes. Press START/STOP to begin preheating.

4.   When the unit has preheated, insert the air fryer basket on Level 3 and place the sheet pan on the wire rack to catch any drippings. Close the oven door to begin cooking.

5.   Check the poppers after 10 minutes. They are ready when the cheese is bubbling and starting to brown. When cooking is complete, remove the basket from the oven.

Onion Ring Fritters

Prep time: 45 minutes | Cook time: 20 minutes | Serves 10 to 12

4 large eggs

2 tablespoons soy sauce

3 tablespoons Worcestershire sauce, divided

2 (1-pound / 454-g) bags frozen onion rings, roughly chopped

1 (6-ounce / 170-g) bag shredded Parmesan cheese

Kosher salt, to taste

1 (1-ounce / 28-g) packet onion soup mix, divided

1 cup mayonnaise

1.   In a small bowl, whisk the eggs with the soy sauce and 2 tablespoons of Worcestershire sauce.

2.   In a large bowl, combine the chopped onion rings, Parmesan, salt, and half of the onion soup mix. Pour the egg mixture evenly over the top, then use your clean hands to toss and mix together. Allow the mixture to sit at room temperature for 30 minutes to allow the frozen onion rings to soften.

3.   Using your hands or a 2-ounce (57-g) ice cream scoop, form the batter into 2-ounce (57-g) balls.

4.   Place the fritters 2 inches apart in the air fryer basket. They should all fit.

5.   Install a wire rack on Level 1. Place a sheet pan with the roast tray set into it on the wire rack. This will catch some of the drippings from the fritters and prevent the oven from smoking. Select AIR FRY, set the temperature to 360ºF (182ºC), and set the time to 20 minutes. Press START/STOP to begin preheating.

6.   When the unit has preheated, insert the air fryer basket on Level 3. Close the oven door to begin cooking.

7.   While the fritters are cooking, combine the remaining onion soup mix with the mayonnaise and remaining 1 tablespoon of Worcestershire sauce in a small bowl. Mix well.

8.   When cooking is complete, serve the fritters with the mayo dipping sauce.

Avocado Crab Rangoon

Prep time: 15 minutes | Cook time: 10 minutes | Serves 6 to 8

8 ounces (227 g) imitation crabmeat

2 ripe Hass avocados, mashed well

1 (8-ounce / 227-g) container whipped cream cheese

½ cup chopped scallions, green parts only

30 square wonton wrappers

Canola oil cooking spray

Sweet chili sauce, for serving

1. In a large bowl, combine the crabmeat, avocados, cream cheese, and scallions. Mix until well combined.

2. On a large, clean workspace, and working in batches if necessary, lay out the wonton wrappers. Fill a small bowl with water.

3. Spoon 1 to 2 tablespoons of the cream cheese mixture on center of a wrapper. Dip a finger in the water and trace the edges of the wonton wrapper. Carefully bring the edges of the wrapper together to form a triangle and pinch firmly to secure. Repeat with the remaining wrappers and filling.

4. Arrange the wontons in a single layer in the air fryer basket. Liberally spray both sides of each wonton with the canola oil.

5. Select AIR FRY, set the temperature to 375ºF (191ºC), and set the time to 10 minutes. Press START/STOP to begin preheating.

6. Once the unit has preheated, insert the air fryer basket on Level 3. Close the oven door to begin cooking.

7. When cooking is complete, remove the basket from the oven and let the wontons cool slightly before serving. Serve with sweet chili sauce.

Kung Pao Chicken and Water Chestnut Totchos

Prep time: 10 minutes | Cook time: 35 minutes | Serves 6 to 8

2 red bell peppers, seeded and cut into 2-inch pieces

1 teaspoon canola oil

1 (2-pound / 907-g) bag frozen tater tots

4 grilled chicken breasts (1 pound / 454 g total), cut into 1-inch pieces

1 cup gluten-free kung pao sauce

1 cup roasted peanuts, chopped, divided

1 (8-ounce / 227-g) can water chestnuts, drained and roughly chopped

1 (6-ounce / 170-g) bag shredded Mozzarella cheese

3 scallions, white and green parts, thinly sliced

1.	In a small bowl, toss the peppers with the canola oil. Place the peppers and tater tots in the air fryer basket.

2.	Ensure no wire racks are installed in the oven. Select AIR FRY, set the temperature to 360ºF (182ºC), and set the time to 35 minutes. Press START/STOP to begin preheating.

3.	When the unit has preheated, insert the air fryer basket on Level 3. Close the oven door to begin cooking.

4.	Put the chicken, kung pao sauce, ½ cup of peanuts, and the water chestnuts in a large bowl, and mix to combine.

5.	When there are 10 minutes remining, remove the basket from the oven. Scoop the chicken mixture over the tots and peppers evenly. Sprinkle the cheese over the top.

6.	Place the basket back in the oven on Level 3, then close the oven door to resume cooking.

7.	When cooking is complete, remove the basket from the oven. Garnish with the remaining peanuts and the scallions.

Braised Chinese Flavor Chicken Wings

Prep time: 10 minutes | Cook time: 1 hour 30 minutes | Serves 6

3 cups soy sauce

2 tablespoons minced fresh ginger

6 garlic cloves, minced

2 tablespoons dark brown sugar

¼ cup rice wine

1 tablespoon Chinese five-spice powder

3 scallions, white and green parts, chopped

2 tablespoons sesame oil

3 pounds (1.4 kg) chicken wings

1.   In a large bowl, whisk together the soy sauce, ginger, garlic, brown sugar, rice wine, five-spice powder, scallions, and sesame oil.

2.   Place the chicken wings in the casserole dish. Pour the marinade evenly over the wings. Cover the dish with plastic wrap and refrigerate for at least 30 minutes but ideally for 6 hours.

3.   Install the wire rack on Level 3. Select AIR ROAST, set the temperature to 300ºF (149ºC), and set the time to 1 hour, 30 minutes. Press START/STOP to begin preheating.

4.   When the unit has preheated, unwrap the dish and place it on the wire rack. Close the oven door to begin cooking.

5.   When cooking is complete, serve the chicken wings in the casserole dish.

Beef Jerky

Prep time: 10 minutes | Cook time: 5 to 6 hours | Serves 4 to 6

¼ cup soy sauce

2 tablespoons Worcestershire sauce

Juice of 2 limes

2 tablespoons dark brown sugar

2 tablespoons chili garlic paste

1½ pounds (680 g) beef eye of round, cut into ¼-inch-thick slices

1. In a small bowl, whisk together the soy sauce, Worcestershire sauce, lime juice, brown sugar, and chili garlic paste.

2. Place the sliced meat in a large resealable plastic bag and pour in the marinade. Seal the bag and massage it to coat the meat evenly. Marinate in the refrigerator for a minimum of 8 hours.

3. Once marinated, remove the meat and discard the excess marinade. Lay the meat slices flat in the air fryer basket in a single layer, without any slices touching each other.

4. Install a wire rack on Level 2 and place a sheet pan on it to catch any drippings. Select DEHYDRATE, set the temperature to 155ºF (68ºC), and set the time to 6 hours. Press START/STOP to begin preheating.

5. When the unit has preheated, insert the air fryer basket on Level 4. Close the oven door to begin dehydrating.

6. After 5 hours, check the jerky for desired doneness. Jerky will be softer with less dehydrating time.

7. Cool the jerky completely. Store in an airtight container.

CHAPTER 4: POULTRY

Orange Whole Chicken with Sweet Potatoes

Prep time: 10 minutes | Cook time: 55 minutes | Serves 6 to 8

8 tablespoons (1 stick) unsalted butter, at room temperature

Grated zest and juice of 1 orange

2 tablespoons fresh rosemary, chopped

2 teaspoons kosher salt, divided

2 teaspoons freshly ground black pepper, divided

1 (5-pound / 2.3-kg) whole chicken, patted dry

3 large sweet potatoes, cut into 1-inch-thick wedges

1 tablespoon canola oil

1.   In a medium bowl, combine the butter, orange zest and juice, rosemary, 1 teaspoon of salt, and 1 teaspoon of pepper and mix well.

2.   Place the chicken on a cutting board. Rub the outside of the chicken with the butter mixture. Let the chicken marinate in the refrigerator for 1 hour.

3.   Put the sweet potatoes in a large bowl and toss with the canola oil and remaining 1 teaspoon of salt and remaining 1 teaspoon of pepper. Place the sweet potatoes in the air fryer basket in a single layer.

4.   Place the chicken on the roast tray nested into a sheet pan.

5.   Install the wire rack on Level 1. Select WHOLE ROAST, select 2 LEVEL, set the temperature to 375ºF (191ºC), and set the time to 55 minutes. Press START/STOP to begin preheating.

6.   When the unit has preheated, place the sheet pan with the roast pan on the wire rack. Insert the air fryer basket on Level 4. Close the oven door to begin cooking.

7.   Cooking is complete when an instant-read thermometer inserted into the chicken reads 165ºF (74ºC). Remove the chicken and potatoes from the oven. Let the chicken rest at least 10 minutes before carving and serving.

Korean Fried Whole Chicken

Prep time: 20 minutes | Cook time: 35 minutes | Serves 4 to 6

1 (5-pound / 2.3-kg) whole chicken, cut into serving pieces (drumsticks, thighs, breasts)

2 tablespoons rice vinegar

2 tablespoons kosher salt

1 tablespoon freshly ground black pepper

1 tablespoon ground ginger

1 cup cornstarch

¼ cup honey

3 tablespoons ketchup

2 tablespoons Korean chili paste (gochujang)

2 tablespoons soy sauce

Canola oil cooking spray

1.   In a large bowl, toss the chicken pieces with the rice vinegar, salt, pepper, and ginger. Working in batches, liberally coat all the pieces in the cornstarch, shaking off any excess. Set aside.

2.   In a separate bowl, whisk together the honey, ketchup, chili paste, and soy sauce until smooth. Set aside.

3.   Install a wire rack on Level 2. Select AIR FRY, set the temperature to 350ºF (177ºC), and set the time to 15 minutes. Press START/STOP to begin preheating.

4.   Arrange the chicken in the air fryer basket. Liberally spray both sides of each piece with canola oil.

5.   When the unit has preheated, nest the roast tray in the sheet pan and place on the wire rack to catch any drippings. Insert the air fryer basket on Level 3. Close the oven door to begin cooking.

6.   After 15 minutes, remove the basket, sheet pan, and roast tray, and let the chicken cool for 20 to 30 minutes. Once cool, spray the chicken again with canola oil.

7.   Select AIR FRY, set the temperature to 375ºF (191ºC), and set the time to 20 minutes. Press START/STOP to begin preheating.

8.   When the unit has preheated, return the sheet pan and roast tray to the wire rack and insert the air fryer basket on Level 3. Close the oven door to begin cooking.

9.   Cooking is complete when an instant-read thermometer inserted into the chicken reads 165ºF (74ºC). Remove the chicken and immediately toss the pieces in the reserved sauce, or serve the sauce on the side. Serve immediately.

Spinach and Ham Chicken Cordon Bleu

Prep time: 10 minutes | Cook time: 30 minutes | Serves 8

8 (6- to 8-ounce / 170- to 227-g) boneless, skinless chicken breasts, pounded thin (about ½ inch thick)

Kosher salt and freshly ground black pepper, to taste

1 teaspoon garlic powder

1 teaspoon onion powder

1 teaspoon paprika

16 slices Swiss cheese

16 slices deli honey ham

Oil, for drizzling

1 (8-ounce / 227-g) package cream cheese, at room temperature

1 (10-ounce / 283-g) package frozen spinach, thawed and well drained

½ medium white onion, finely chopped

1 teaspoon Dijon mustard

¼ teaspoon ground nutmeg

½ cup whole milk

1.   Sprinkle the pounded chicken breasts on both sides with salt and pepper, the garlic powder, onion powder, and paprika.

2.   Layer 1 slice of Swiss cheese, 2 slices of ham, then 1 more slice of Swiss cheese on top of each chicken breast. Roll up each piece of chicken and secure it with a toothpick.

3.   Place the chicken on one sheet pan and top with a drizzle of oil.

4.   Install the wire racks on Levels 1 and 3. Select AIR ROAST, select 2 LEVEL, set the temperature to 375ºF (191ºC), and set the time to 30 minutes. Press START/STOP to begin preheating.

5.   When the unit has preheated, place the sheet pan with the chicken on the wire rack on Level 3. Close the oven door to begin cooking.

6.   In a medium bowl, mix together the cream cheese, spinach, onion, mustard, and nutmeg. Spread the mixture evenly on the other sheet pan. After 20 minutes have passed, place the sheet pan with spinach mixture on the wire rack on Level 1, and cook along with the chicken for the remaining 10 minutes.

7.   Remove the spinach mixture from the oven, transfer it in a bowl, and whisk in the milk to thin and create a sauce. Set aside.

8.   Cooking is complete when an instant-read thermometer inserted in the chicken reads 165ºF (74ºC). Remove the pan from the oven and top the chicken with the spinach sauce.

Crispy Chicken Po' Boys with Coleslaw

Prep time: 20 minutes | Cook time: 30 minutes | Serves 6

5 (8-ounce / 227-g) boneless, skinless chicken breasts, cut lengthwise into 1-inch-wide strips

2½ cups buttermilk

8 tablespoons hot sauce, divided

5 tablespoons Cajun seasoning, divided

2 cups all-purpose flour

Kosher salt and freshly ground black pepper, to taste

Coleslaw Mix:

½ cup mayonnaise

¼ cup apple cider vinegar

¼ cup Dijon mustard

2 tablespoons dill pickle brine

3 (12-inch) baguettes

1.　To make the chicken: Put the chicken strips, buttermilk, 6 tablespoons of hot sauce, and 1 tablespoon of Cajun seasoning into a resealable freezer bag. Mix until fully incorporated and the chicken is coated. Seal and refrigerate for at least 6 hours or overnight.

2.　Remove the chicken from the marinade and strain over the sink to drain any excess liquid.

3.　In a medium bowl, whisk together the flour, remaining 4 tablespoons of Cajun seasoning, salt, and pepper. Dredge the chicken strips in the seasoned flour, gently shaking off any excess. Place the strips in the air fryer basket.

4.　Install a wire rack on Level 1. Select AIR FRY, select 2 LEVEL, set the temperature to 360ºF (182ºC), and set the time to 30 minutes. Press START/STOP to begin preheating.

5.　When the unit has preheated, insert the air fryer basket on Level 3. Close the oven door to begin cooking.

6.　To make the remoulade coleslaw: While the chicken is cooking, combine the coleslaw mix, mayonnaise, vinegar, mustard, pickle brine, remaining 2 tablespoons of hot sauce, salt, and pepper in a medium bowl and set aside.

7.　When there are 5 minutes remaining, place the baguettes on the sheet pan. Place the sheet pan on the wire rack on Level 1, and cook along with the chicken for the remaining 5 minutes.

8.　Cooking is complete when an instant-read thermometer inserted in the chicken reads 165ºF (74ºC) and the exterior is crispy.

9.　Carefully remove the bread and chicken from the oven. Let the bread cool for a few minutes. Cut the baguettes into top and bottom halves. Top the bottom halves with the chicken, slaw, and any desired toppings, then cover with the top baguette halves. Cut each sandwich crosswise to serve.

Chicken Fajitas

Prep time: 10 minutes | Cook time: 20 minutes | Serves 4 to 6

Cooking oil spray

1½ pounds (680 g) boneless, skinless chicken breasts, cut into ½-inch-thick strips

1 green bell pepper, seeded and sliced

1 red bell pepper, seeded and sliced

1 medium red onion, halved lengthwise, then sliced crosswise

3 garlic cloves, minced

Juice of 2 limes

3 tablespoons canola oil

2 teaspoons chili powder

1½ teaspoons ground cumin

1 teaspoon paprika

1 teaspoon garlic powder

½ teaspoon kosher salt

½ teaspoon freshly ground black pepper

Tortillas, for serving

1. Lightly coat a sheet pan with cooking spray and set aside.
2. Place the chicken, bell peppers, and onion in a large bowl. Add the garlic, lime juice, and oil and toss to coat evenly.
3. Sprinkle the chili powder, cumin, paprika, garlic powder, salt, and pepper over the chicken mixture and toss again to coat evenly. Spread the fajita mixture in an even layer on the sheet pan.
4. Install a wire rack on Level 3. Select AIR ROAST, set the temperature to 400ºF (204ºC), and set the time for 20 minutes. Press START/STOP to begin preheating.
5. When the unit has preheated, place the sheet pan on the wire rack. Close the oven door to begin cooking.
6. After 10 minutes, remove the pan and toss the fajitas using tongs. Return the pan to the oven to finish cooking.
7. Cooking is complete when an instant-read thermometer inserted into the chicken reads 165ºF (74ºC). Serve warm with tortillas and desired toppings.

Honey Chicken with Potato Wedges

Prep time: 15 minutes | Cook time: 20 minutes | Serves 4

2 russet potatoes, cut into 2-inch-thick wedges
2 cups ice cubes
¼ cup Dijon mustard
¼ cup plain yogurt or sour cream
2 tablespoons honey
1½ pounds (680 g) boneless, skinless chicken breasts
2 cups finely crushed salted pretzels
1 teaspoon onion powder
1¼ teaspoons garlic powder, divided
1 teaspoon smoked paprika, divided
½ teaspoon freshly ground black pepper, divided
2 tablespoons extra-virgin olive oil
1 teaspoon kosher salt

1.   Place the potato wedges in a large bowl and cover them with cold water and ice cubes. Let them soak for at least 30 minutes, then drain and pat dry with paper towels.
2.   In a large bowl, whisk together the mustard, yogurt, and honey. Add the chicken to the mixture and toss to evenly coat. Let sit for 30 minutes.
3.   Meanwhile, in a medium bowl, combine the crushed pretzels, onion powder, 1 teaspoon of garlic powder, ½ teaspoon of paprika, and ¼ teaspoon of black pepper.
4.   Line a sheet pan with parchment paper. Remove each piece of chicken from the honey mustard and dredge it through the pretzel mixture, pressing gently to ensure the crumbs adhere, then place it on the prepared sheet pan.
5.   In the bowl used to soak the potatoes, whisk together the olive oil, remaining ½ teaspoon of paprika, remaining ¼ teaspoon of garlic powder, the salt, and the remaining ¼ teaspoon of black pepper. Add the potato wedges and toss to coat. Arrange the potatoes evenly in the air fryer basket.
6.   Install a wire rack on Level 1. Select AIR FRY, select 2 LEVEL, set the temperature to 400ºF (204ºC), and set the time to 28 minutes. Press START/STOP to begin preheating.
7.   When the unit has preheated, place the sheet pan on the wire rack and insert the air fryer basket on Level 4. Close the oven door to begin cooking.
8.   Cooking is complete when an instant-read thermometer inserted into the chicken reads 165ºF (74ºC) and the potato wedges are cooked to your desired crispiness. Serve hot.

Chicken Tacos

Prep time: 10 minutes | Cook time: 30 minutes | Serves 4 to 6

1 tablespoon extra-virgin olive oil

1 small onion, sliced

2 garlic cloves, minced

1 tablespoon kosher salt

1 teaspoon ground cumin

½ teaspoon ground cinnamon

3 or 4 boneless, skinless chicken breasts (about 2½ pounds / 1.1 kg total), cut into thin strips

1 (14.5-ounce / 411-g) can fire-roasted diced tomatoes

2 tablespoons chopped mild green chiles

2 tablespoons tomato paste

½ teaspoon smoked paprika

2 tablespoons freshly squeezed lime juice

10 flat-bottomed corn taco shells

1 lime, cut into wedges

1 cup sour cream

1½ cups shredded Mexican-blend cheese

1. Put the olive oil, onion, garlic, salt, cumin, cinnamon, and chicken strips on a sheet pan. Gently toss to combine.

2. Install a wire rack on Level 3. Select AIR ROAST, set the temperature to 400ºF (204ºC), and set the time to 28 minutes. Press START/STOP to begin preheating.

3. When the unit has preheated, place the sheet pan on the wire rack. Close the oven door to begin cooking.

4. While the chicken is cooking, combine the tomatoes with their juices, chiles, tomato paste, paprika, and lime juice in a small bowl. Set aside.

5. When there are 15 minutes remaining, remove the pan from the oven and drain any excess liquid. Gently pour the tomato mixture over the chicken and return the sheet pan to the oven. Close the oven door to resume cooking.

6. Meanwhile, line up the taco shells in the casserole dish.

7. When cooking is complete, remove the sheet pan from the oven. Using tongs, place a bit of chicken in each taco shell. Squeeze a bit of lime juice from the lime wedges over each taco, spoon a bit of sour cream in each, then sprinkle with the cheese.

8. Select BROIL, set the temperature to HI, and set the time to 2 minutes. Press START/STOP to begin.

9. Place the sheet pan on the wire rack and close the door to begin cooking. Broil until the cheese is melted, adding more time if necessary.

10. Serve with your favorite taco toppings.

Chicken and Cannellini Bean Stew

Prep time: 15 minutes | Cook time: 1 hour | Serves 6

Meat from 1 rotisserie chicken, roughly shredded

1 (12-ounce / 340-g) package precooked chicken sausages, sliced

3 medium carrots, diced

1 (16-ounce / 454-g) bag frozen pearl onions

1 (15-ounce / 425-g) can cannellini beans, drained and rinsed

3 garlic cloves, minced

2 cups chicken stock

Kosher salt and freshly ground black pepper, to taste

1.   In a large bowl, combine the chicken, sausages, carrots, pearl onions, beans, garlic, stock, salt, and pepper. Pour the mixture into a casserole dish.

2.   Install a wire rack on Level 3. Select AIR ROAST, set the temperature to 325ºF (163ºC), and set the time to 60 minutes. Press START/STOP to begin preheating.

3.   When the unit has preheated, place the casserole dish on the wire rack. Close the oven door to begin cooking.

4.   When cooking is complete, let the stew cool for 10 minutes before serving.

Chicken Enchiladas

Prep time: 15 minutes | Cook time: 25 minutes | Serves 4

2 to 3 cups shredded cooked chicken

2 cups shredded Monterey Jack cheese, divided

1 (4.5-ounce / 128-g) can chopped green chiles

Kosher salt and freshly ground black pepper, to taste

1 cup sour cream

8 (10-inch) flour tortillas

1 (8-ounce / 227-g) jar green chile enchilada sauce

1.	In a medium bowl, combine the chicken, 1 cup of cheese, the green chiles, salt, and pepper.

2.	Spoon $^1/_3$ cup of the chicken mixture and 2 tablespoons of sour cream down the middle of each tortilla. Roll up the tortillas and place them seam-side down in a casserole dish. Pour the enchilada sauce over the tortillas and top with remaining 1 cup of cheese.

3.	Install a wire rack on Level 3. Select AIR ROAST, set the temperature to 350ºF (177ºC), and set the time to 25 minutes. Press START/STOP to begin preheating.

4.	When the unit has preheated, place the casserole dish on the wire rack. Close the oven door to begin cooking.

5.	When cooking is complete, let the enchiladas cool for 10 minutes before serving.

Chicken and Gouda Casserole

Prep time: 15 minutes | Cook time: 35 minutes | Serves 6 to 8

2 (10.5-ounce / 298-g) cans cream of chicken soup

2 cups chicken stock

2 cups chopped cooked chicken breast

1 cup grated Parmesan cheese

1 cup shredded Gouda cheese

Kosher salt and freshly ground black pepper, to taste

½ cup panko bread crumbs

4 tablespoons (½ stick) unsalted butter, melted

1. In a large bowl, combine the soup, stock, chicken breast, Parmesan, Gouda, salt, and pepper. Transfer the mixture to a casserole dish.

2. Install a wire rack on Level 3. Select BAKE, set the temperature to 375ºF (191ºC), and set the time to 35 minutes. Press START/STOP to begin preheating.

3. When the unit has preheated, place the casserole dish on the wire rack. Close the oven door to begin cooking.

4. In a small bowl, mix together the panko bread crumbs and melted butter. After the chicken has cooked for 30 minutes, spoon the panko bread crumbs over the top of the casserole. Continue cooking for the remaining 5 minutes.

5. When cooking is complete, let the casserole cool for 10 minutes before serving.

Mexican Turkey Meatloaf

Prep time: 15 minutes | Cook time: 45 minutes | Serves 6 to 8

For the Meatloaf:

Cooking oil spray

2 pounds (907 g) ground turkey

$^1/_3$ cup salsa

1 cup quick-cooking oats

2 large eggs

1 (4-ounce / 113-g) can chopped green chiles

$^1/_3$ cup chopped fresh cilantro, divided

1 (1-ounce / 28-g) packet taco seasoning

1 (15-ounce / 425-g) can red enchilada sauce, divided

$^1/_3$ cup ketchup

Kosher salt and freshly ground black pepper, to taste

For the Corn:

6 ears corn, shucked

3 tablespoons butter, at room temperature

2 teaspoons chili powder

Salt and freshly ground black pepper to taste

¼ cup plain Greek yogurt

¼ cup crumbled cotija cheese

Lime wedges, for serving

1.   To make the meatloaf: Line a sheet pan with parchment paper and spray the parchment with cooking spray.

2.   In a large bowl, combine the turkey, salsa, oats, eggs, green chiles, half of the cilantro, the taco seasoning, and half of the enchilada sauce. Mix until well combined.

3.   Transfer the meat mixture to the prepared pan and form it into cylinder about 5 inches wide.

4.   In a small bowl, whisk together the remaining half of the enchilada sauce and the ketchup, and season with salt and pepper to taste. Evenly glaze the top of the meatloaf, reserving half for a second glaze.

5.   Install the wire racks on Levels 1 and 3. Select AIR ROAST, select 2 LEVEL, set the temperature to 350ºF (177ºC), and set the time to 45 minutes. Press START/STOP to begin preheating.

6.   Once the unit has preheated, place the sheet pan on Level 3. Close the oven to begin cooking.

7.   To make the corn: On a separate sheet pan, place a piece of foil that is long enough to wrap the 6 ears of corn.

8.   Rub the corn evenly with the butter. Season the ears all over with the chili powder, salt, and pepper. Wrap all the corn in the foil, creating a foil package.

9.   When there are 30 minutes remaining, place the sheet pan with the corn on the lower wire rack. Glaze the meatloaf again with the remaining glaze and continue cooking for the remaining 30 minutes.

10.   Cooking is complete when an instant-read thermometer inserted in the center reads 165ºF (74ºC). Let the meatloaf rest for 5 to 10 minutes before slicing.

11.   Remove the corn from the oven and open the foil packet. Slather the corn with the yogurt and sprinkle with the cheese. Serve alongside the meatloaf with the lime wedges and remaining cilantro on the side.

CHAPTER 5: BEEF, PORK, AND LAMB

Easy Carne Asada Tacos

Prep time: 15 minutes | Cook time: 15 minutes | Serves 4 to 6

2 tablespoons soy sauce

Juice of 2 limes

2 tablespoons avocado oil, divided

4 garlic cloves, minced

2 teaspoons chili powder

1 teaspoon ground cumin

½ teaspoon salt

¼ teaspoon freshly ground black pepper

1½ pounds (680 g) skirt steak or flank steak

12 corn tortillas

1 small red onion, diced

1 jalapeño, sliced

½ cup chopped fresh cilantro

1. In a medium bowl, whisk together the soy sauce, lime juice, avocado oil, garlic, chili powder, cumin, salt, and pepper. Pour the marinade into a large resealable bag. Add the steak, seal the bag, and marinate in the refrigerator for 1 hour.

2. Remove the steak from the marinade (discarding any liquid) and place it in the center of the sheet pan.

3. Install a wire rack on Level 4. Select BROIL, set the temperature to HI, and set the time to 15 minutes. Press START/STOP to begin. Place the sheet pan on the wire rack and close the door to begin cooking.

4. When cooking is complete, transfer the steak to a cutting board and let it rest for 10 minutes before slicing.

5. Divide the sliced steak among the tortillas, then topping with the onion, jalapeño, and cilantro.

Flank Steak with Roasted Brussels Sprouts

Prep time: 10 minutes | Cook time: 15 minutes | Serves 4 to 6

¼ cup mayonnaise

3 tablespoons grated Parmesan cheese

2 garlic cloves, crushed

1 tablespoon freshly squeezed lemon juice

2 tablespoons panko bread crumbs

2 pounds (907 g) flank steak

12 ounces (340 g) Brussels sprouts, halved

2 red bell peppers, seeded and cut into 1-inch pieces

½ red onion, cut into 1-inch pieces

3 tablespoons vegetable oil

Kosher salt and freshly ground black pepper, to taste

1. In a small bowl, combine the mayonnaise, Parmesan cheese, garlic, lemon juice, and panko bread crumbs. Spread the mixture evenly over the top of the steak. Place the steak on the sheet pan.

2. In a large bowl, toss the Brussels sprouts, bell peppers, and onion with the oil. Season with salt and pepper. Place the vegetables in a single layer in the air fryer basket.

3. Install a wire rack on Level 1. Select AIR ROAST, select 2 LEVEL, set the temperature to 425ºF (218ºC), and set the time to 15 minutes. Press START/STOP to begin preheating.

4. When the unit has preheated, place the sheet pan on the wire rack, and insert the air fryer basket on Level 3. Close the oven door to begin cooking.

5. When cooking is complete, remove the meat and vegetables from the oven. Let the meat rest for at least 5 minutes before slicing.

Barbecue Beef Meatloaf with Potato Cubes

Prep time: 5 minutes | Cook time: 55 minutes | Serves 6

For the Meatloaf:

1½ pounds (680 g) ground beef

2 tablespoons minced garlic

1 medium white onion, finely chopped

½ cup panko bread crumbs

1 large egg

1 cup prepared barbecue sauce, divided

2 tablespoons yellow mustard

2 tablespoons barbecue seasoning

Kosher salt and freshly ground black pepper, to taste

5 bacon slices, halved crosswise

For the Potatoes:

4 russet potatoes, peeled and cut into 1-inch cubes

2 tablespoons canola oil

1 teaspoon kosher salt

1 (1-ounce / 28-g) packet ranch dressing mix

Cooking oil spray

¼ cup grated Parmesan cheese

1 tablespoon chopped fresh parsley

1. To make the meatloaf: In a large bowl, mix together the ground beef, garlic, onion, panko bread crumbs, egg, ½ cup of barbecue sauce, mustard, and barbecue seasoning until well combined. Season with salt and pepper to taste.

2. Place the mixture on the sheet pan and form it into a rounded football-like shape. Lay the bacon slices over the top, covering the meatloaf from end to end.

3. To make the potatoes: In a separate large bowl, toss the potatoes with the canola oil, salt, and ranch dressing mix. Spray the air fryer basket with cooking oil and place the potatoes in the basket.

4. Install a wire rack on Level 1. Select AIR ROAST, select 2 LEVEL, set the temperature to 400ºF (204ºC), and set the time to 55 minutes. Press START/STOP to begin preheating.

5. When the unit has preheated, place the sheet pan on the wire rack, and insert the air fryer basket on Level 3. Close the oven door to begin cooking.

6. When 10 minutes remain, remove the meatloaf and brush the remaining ½ cup of barbecue sauce over the meatloaf. Remove the air fryer basket and toss the potatoes with the Parmesan. Return the meatloaf and potatoes to the oven and continue cooking.

7. When cooking is complete, an instant-read thermometer inserted into the meatloaf should read at least 155ºF (68ºC).

8. Toss the potatoes with the parsley, and let the meatloaf rest for about 5 minutes before slicing and serving.

Honey Pork with Beans and Potatoes

Prep time: 15 minutes | Cook time: 25 minutes | Serves 8 to 12

6 tablespoons balsamic vinegar

¼ cup honey

2½ tablespoons extra-virgin olive oil

2 teaspoons minced garlic

4 teaspoons minced rosemary

2 pork tenderloins (2 to 2½ pounds / 907 g to 1.1 kg in total)

Kosher salt and freshly ground black pepper, to taste

1 pound (454 g) green beans, trimmed

1 pound (454 g) baby red potatoes, halved

1 large red onion, thinly sliced

1. In a small bowl, whisk together the balsamic vinegar, honey, olive oil, garlic, and rosemary. Set aside.

2. Pat the pork tenderloins dry with paper towels. Season with salt and pepper and place them on the roast tray set into a sheet pan. Brush or spoon the balsamic mixture over the tenderloins, reserving about ¼ cup.

3. In a large bowl, combine the green beans, potatoes, and onion and season with salt and pepper. Add the reserved balsamic mixture to the bowl and toss to evenly coat the vegetables. Arrange the vegetables on the other sheet pan in an even layer.

4. Install the wire racks on Levels 1 and 4. Select AIR ROAST, select 2 LEVEL, set the temperature to 425ºF (218ºC), and set the time to 25 minutes. Press START/STOP to begin preheating.

5. When the unit has preheated, place the sheet pan with the meat on Level 1 and the vegetables on Level 4. Close the oven door to begin cooking.

6. When cooking is complete, an instant-read thermometer inserted into the pork should read at least 145ºF (63ºC) and the vegetables should be fork-tender.

7. Let the meat rest for about 5 minutes before slicing and serving.

Pork Wellington

Prep time: 15 minutes | Cook time: 45 minutes | Serves 4 to 6

1 pound (454 g) green beans, trimmed

2 tablespoons extra-virgin olive oil

2 garlic cloves, minced

Kosher salt and freshly ground black pepper, to taste

All-purpose flour, for dusting

1 frozen puff pastry sheet, thawed and rolled out to 12 by 15 inches

¼ cup apricot preserves

½ teaspoon dried thyme

4 thin slices prosciutto

1 (1½- to 2-pound / 680- to 907-g) pork tenderloin, silver skin removed

2 tablespoons whole-grain mustard

2 tablespoons Dijon mustard

1 large egg, beaten with 1 tablespoon water

1.   In a large bowl, toss the green beans with the olive oil, garlic, salt, and pepper. Set aside.

2.   Dust a clean work surface with flour and lay out the puff pastry. Gently spread the apricot preserves over the middle 2 quarters. Sprinkle with the thyme and a pinch of salt and pepper.

3.   Layer the prosciutto on top of the preserves lengthwise; you want the prosciutto to wrap around the whole tenderloin.

4.   Place the tenderloin on a cutting board and pat dry with paper towels. Rub the whole-grain and Dijon mustards all over the meat and season it with salt and pepper. Place the tenderloin gently on the prosciutto, pushing in on both ends of the meat to ensure the tenderloin has even thickness throughout. Leave a 2-inch border of puff pastry on each end.

5.   Fold one side of the puff pastry over the top of the tenderloin and roll to enclose the meat tightly. Brush a bit of the egg wash on the seam to seal. Turn the Wellington so it is seam-side down. Tightly close the ends and use the egg wash to seal completely. Finally, brush all over with the egg wash to promote even browning during cooking.

6.   Place the Wellington on the sheet pan seam-side down. Place the green beans on both sides of the Wellington.

7.   Install a wire rack on Level 2. Select AIR ROAST, set the temperature to 350ºF (177ºC), and set the time to 45 minutes. Press START/STOP to begin preheating.

8.   When the unit has preheated, place the sheet pan on the wire rack. Close the oven door to begin cooking.

9.   Cooking is complete when the puff pastry is golden brown and an instant-read thermometer inserted into the pork reads at least 145ºF (63ºC).

Cuban Pork with Fried Plantains

Prep time: 15 minutes | Cook time: 2 hours 10 minutes | Serves 6 to 8

1 small white onion, diced

5 garlic cloves, crushed

1 tablespoon dried oregano, preferably Mexican

1 tablespoon kosher salt

1 teaspoon freshly ground black pepper

2 cups freshly squeezed orange juice

1 cup freshly squeezed lime juice

3 pounds (1.4 kg) boneless pork shoulder

2 cups water

4 overripe (nearly black) plantains, peeled and sliced on the diagonal

Cooking oil spray

1. In a blender, combine the onion, garlic, oregano, salt, pepper, orange juice, and lime juice. Blend until frothy. Reserve 1 cup of marinade and pour the rest into a resealable bag. Add the pork, seal the bag, and make sure the meat is thoroughly coated. Refrigerate overnight.

2. Pour the contents of the bag (meat and liquid) into the casserole dish, add the water, and cover tightly with foil.

3. Install a wire rack on Level 1. Select WHOLE ROAST, set the temperature to 300ºF (149ºC), and set the time to 2 hours. Press START/STOP to begin preheating.

4. When the unit has preheated, place the covered casserole dish on the wire rack. Close the oven door to begin cooking.

5. When the pork is fork-tender, carefully remove the foil but leave the roast in the oven.

6. Select AIR FRY, select 2 LEVEL, set the temperature to 400ºF (204ºC), and set the time to 10 minutes.

7. Arrange the sliced plantains in the air fryer basket. Generously spray with cooking oil, then insert the air fryer basket on Level 3. Press START/STOP to begin cooking.

8. Cooking is complete when the plantains are caramelized and an instant-read thermometer inserted into the pork reads at least 205ºF (96ºC). Serve with the reserved mojo marinade.

Mojito Pulled Pork Burgers

Prep time: 30 minutes | Cook time: 2 hours 30 minutes | Serves 6

¼ cup white rum
Juice of 4 limes
Juice of 2 oranges
4 garlic cloves, minced
1 teaspoon ground cumin
4 tablespoons chopped fresh mint
4 tablespoons chopped fresh oregano
4 tablespoons chopped fresh cilantro
Kosher salt and freshly ground black pepper, to taste
2 pounds (907 g) boneless pork butt, cut into 2-inch chunks
6 burger buns, split
Pickled jalapeño, dill pickle chips, thinly sliced red onion, and slaw, for serving

1.   In a small bowl, combine the rum, lime juice, orange juice, garlic, cumin, mint, oregano, and cilantro. Season with salt and pepper.
2.   Season the pork with salt and pepper and place it in the baking pan. Pour the marinade over the pork. Cover the pan with foil and marinate in the refrigerator for at least 2 hours or up to overnight.
3.   Install the wire racks on Levels 1 and 3. Select AIR ROAST, select 2 LEVEL, set the temperature to 325ºF (163ºC), and set the time to 2 hours 30 minutes. Press START/STOP to begin preheating.
4.   When the unit has preheated, place the covered pan on Level 3. Close the oven door to begin cooking.
5.   When there are 5 minutes remaining, place the buns cut-side up on a sheet pan and place the sheet pan on Level 1.
6.   When cooking is complete, remove the buns and pork from the oven.
7.   Using two forks, pull apart and shred the pork. Place a big scoop of the meat on each bun bottom and top the burgers with the other half of the bun. Serve with the pickled jalapeño, dill pickle chips, thinly sliced red onion, and slaw as desired.

Chorizo and Cauliflower Rice Stuffed Peppers

Prep time: 10 minutes | Cook time: 40 minutes | Serves 6 to 8

1 pound (454 g) chorizo sausage, diced

2 (12-ounce / 340-g) bags cauliflower rice

1 (16-ounce / 454-g) jar black bean salsa

2 cups shredded sharp Cheddar cheese

8 poblano peppers, halved lengthwise and seeded

1.   In a large bowl, stir together the chorizo, cauliflower rice, salsa, and 1½ cups of cheese until thoroughly combined. Fill each half pepper with the mixture evenly, about 1 cup per half. Arrange the stuffed peppers in the air fryer basket in a single layer.

2.   Install a wire rack on Level 1. Select AIR ROAST, set the temperature to 375ºF (191ºC), and set the time to 35 minutes. Press START/STOP to begin preheating.

3.   When the unit has preheated, place the sheet pan on the wire rack to catch any drippings, and insert the air fryer basket on Level 3. Close the oven door to begin cooking.

4.   When cooking is complete, carefully remove the sheet pan and air fryer basket, and top each pepper with the remaining cheese.

5.   Place the sheet pan back on the wire rack and the air fryer basket on Level 3. Select AIR ROAST, set the temperature to 450ºF (232ºC), and set the time to 5 minutes. Press START/STOP to begin.

6.   When cooking is complete, let the peppers cool for about 5 minutes before serving.

Lamb Rack with Potato Salad

Prep time: 30 minutes | Cook time: 20 to 30 minutes | Serves 4

1 (1½-pound / 680-g) rack of lamb

Kosher salt and freshly ground black pepper, to taste

2 tablespoons canola oil, divided

1½ pounds (680 g) baby Yukon Gold potatoes, halved

¼ cup bread crumbs

2 tablespoons grated Parmesan cheese

1 teaspoon minced fresh thyme

1 teaspoon minced fresh rosemary

4 tablespoons Dijon mustard, divided

½ cup mayonnaise

¼ cup pitted kalamata olives, chopped

1 celery stalk, finely chopped

½ small red onion, finely chopped

2 tablespoons minced fresh dill

Grated zest and juice of 1 lemon

1.   Install the wire racks on Levels 1 and 3. Select AIR ROAST, select 2 LEVEL, set the temperature to 425ºF (218ºC), and set the time to 30 minutes. Press START/STOP to begin preheating.

2.   Place the lamb fat-side up on the roast tray set into a sheet pan. Season the lamb with salt and pepper, and coat it with 1 tablespoon of canola oil.

3.   In a large bowl, toss the potatoes with remaining 1 tablespoon of canola oil and season with salt and pepper. Place in an even layer on the other sheet pan.

4.   When the unit has preheated, place the sheet pan with the lamb on Level 3 and the potatoes on Level 1. Close the oven door to begin cooking.

5.   In a small bowl, mix together the bread crumbs, Parmesan, thyme, rosemary, salt, and pepper.

6.   When there are 20 minutes remaining, reduce the heat to 400ºF (204ºC) and remove the lamb from the oven. Spread 3 tablespoons of mustard on the meat and press on the bread crumb mixture, coating evenly.

7.   Return the lamb to the oven and continue cooking for 10 to 20 minutes, depending on how you like your lamb cooked.

8.   When cooking is complete, remove the lamb and potatoes. Let the lamb rest for 5 to 10 minutes.

9.   Place the potatoes in a large bowl. Add the remaining 1 tablespoon of mustard, the mayonnaise, olives, celery, onion, dill, and lemon zest and juice. Toss to combine.

10.   Slice the lamb between the bones and serve with the potato salad.

CHAPTER 6: SEAFOOD

Cod with Potato Chips

Prep time: 20 minutes | Cook time: 25 minutes | Serves 4

2 large eggs

1 cup ale beer

1 cup cornstarch

1 cup all-purpose flour

½ tablespoon chili powder

1 tablespoon ground cumin

1 teaspoon sea salt, plus more for seasoning

1 teaspoon freshly ground black pepper, plus more for seasoning

4 (5- to 6-ounce / 142- to 170-g) cod fillets

Cooking oil spray

2 large russet potatoes, cut into ¼- to ½-inch-thick sticks

2 tablespoons vegetable oil

1.   In a shallow bowl, whisk together the eggs and beer. In a medium bowl, whisk together the cornstarch, flour, chili powder, cumin, salt, and pepper.

2.   Dip each cod fillet in the egg mixture, then dredge in the flour mixture, coating on all sides.

3.   Coat the sheet pan with cooking spray. Evenly arrange the fish fillets on the pan and lightly spray each with cooking spray.

4.   In a large bowl, toss the potatoes with the vegetable oil and season with salt and pepper.

5.   Coat the air fryer basket with cooking spray. Evenly arrange the potatoes in the basket.

6.   Install a wire rack on Level 3. Select AIR FRY, select 2 LEVEL, set the temperature to 400ºF (204ºC), and set the time to 25 minutes. Press START/STOP to begin preheating.

7.   When the unit has preheated, place the sheet pan on the wire rack and insert the air fryer basket on Level 3. Close the oven door to begin cooking.

8.   When cooking is complete, check for desired crispness. Cook for 5 minutes more if needed.

Tilapia Tacos

Prep time: 20 minutes | Cook time: 10 minutes | Serves 4

1 pound (454 g) tilapia fillets, cut into 1-inch-wide strips

Juice of 1 lime

1 (1-ounce / 28-g) packet taco seasoning

½ cup all-purpose flour

2 large eggs

1 teaspoon sriracha hot sauce

2 cups panko bread crumbs

½ bunch fresh cilantro, minced

½ teaspoon kosher salt

¼ teaspoon freshly ground black pepper

Cooking oil spray

12 corn tortillas, warmed

1.   Place the tilapia strips in a medium bowl. Drizzle them with the lime juice and sprinkle with the taco seasoning. Toss to evenly coat.

2.   Prepare the breading station by laying out three shallow bowls. Put the flour in the first bowl. In the second bowl, whisk together the eggs and sriracha. In the third bowl, combine the panko bread crumbs, cilantro, salt, and pepper.

3.   Lightly coat each fish strip in flour, then dip it in the egg mixture, gently shaking off any excess. Finally, coat each strip in the bread crumb mixture.

4.   Coat the air fryer basket with cooking spray and arrange the breaded fish evenly in the basket, ensuring the fish is not overcrowded. Coat the fish strips with cooking spray.

5.   Select AIR FRY, set the temperature to 425ºF (218ºC), and set the time to 10 minutes. Press START/STOP to begin preheating.

6.   When the unit has preheated, insert the air fryer basket on Level 3. Close the oven door to begin cooking.

7.   When cooking is complete, serve the fish in the corn tortillas with the toppings of your choice.

Whitefish in Foil

Prep time: 20 minutes | Cook time: 20 minutes | Serves 8

Juice of 2 oranges (about 1½ cups)

1 cup chicken broth

1 cup white wine

2 cups Israeli couscous

Kosher salt and freshly ground black pepper, to taste

1 (16-ounce / 454-g) bag frozen mixed vegetables

8 tablespoons chopped Niçoise olives, divided

8 (6-ounce / 170-g) hearty whitefish fillets, such as cod or bass

8 tablespoons (1 stick) cold butter, cut into tablespoons

1.   In a large bowl, combine the orange juice, broth, and wine.

2.   Place 8 foil sheets on the countertop. Bend the corners inward to create a shallow bowl; this will prevent the ingredients from falling out during assembly.

3.   Place ¼ cup of couscous on each foil sheet and season with salt and pepper. Place ½ cup of frozen vegetables on top of the couscous. Place ½ tablespoon of olives on the vegetables.

4.   Place 1 fish fillet on the top, then sprinkle each with ½ tablespoon of olives. Smear gently to cover most of each piece of fish with the olives. Place 1 tablespoon of butter on top of each fish portion and season with salt and pepper.

5.   Divide the orange juice mixture evenly between the packets, pouring it over the fish.

6.   Lift the edges of the foil upward and inward, then fold the edges over one another and crimp to make a seal. Ensure the seal is tight so steam doesn't escape during cooking. Place the foil packets on the sheet pan.

7.   Install a wire rack on Level 1. Select AIR ROAST, set the temperature to 375ºF (191ºC), and set the time to 20 minutes. Press START/STOP to begin preheating.

8.   When the unit has preheated, place the sheet pan on the wire rack. Close the oven door to begin cooking.

9.   When cooking is complete, remove the sheet pan from the oven. Be careful to avoid steam when opening the foil packets. Serve.

Parmesan Tilapia with Asparagus

Prep time: 15 minutes | Cook time: 30 minutes | Serves 6

1 cup grated Parmesan cheese

3 tablespoons chopped fresh parsley

Kosher salt and freshly ground black pepper, to taste

½ cup panko bread crumbs

4 tablespoons (½ stick) unsalted butter, melted

6 (4-ounce / 113-g) tilapia fillets

1 bunch asparagus, woody ends trimmed, cut into 1-inch pieces

1 tablespoon canola oil

1. Combine the Parmesan, parsley, salt and pepper, panko bread crumbs, and melted butter. Mix thoroughly to combine. Press the mixture onto the top of the tilapia fillets.

2. In a separate medium bowl, toss the asparagus and oil until evenly coated. Season with salt and pepper and toss again.

3. Arrange the fillets on the sheet pan with the asparagus around them. Install a wire rack on Level 3. Select AIR ROAST, set the temperature to 375ºF (191ºC), and set the time to 30 minutes. Press START/STOP to begin preheating.

4. When the unit has preheated, place the sheet pan on the wire rack. Close the oven door to begin cooking.

5. When cooking is complete, let the fish cool for 10 minutes before serving.

Mahi-Mahi with Potatoes and Pineapple

Prep time: 15 minutes | Cook time: 25 to 30 minutes | Serves 6

2 cups baby carrots, halved

2 small russet potatoes, peeled and cut into ½-inch sticks

2 tablespoons crushed garlic

3 tablespoons canola oil, divided

1 small pineapple, peeled, cored, and cut into wedges

2 teaspoons curry powder, divided

6 (6-ounce / 170-g) mahi-mahi fillets

Juice of 1 lime

Kosher salt and freshly ground black pepper, to taste

1. In a medium bowl, toss the carrots, potatoes, garlic, and 1 tablespoon of oil until evenly coated. Arrange the vegetables evenly in the air fryer basket.

2. In a separate bowl, toss the pineapple with 1 teaspoon of curry powder and arrange in the basket with the vegetables.

3. Install a wire rack on Level 1. Select AIR FRY, select 2 LEVEL, set the temperature to 455ºF (235ºC), and set the time to 30 minutes. Press START/STOP to begin preheating

4. When the unit has preheated, insert the air fryer basket on Level 3. Close the oven door to begin cooking.

5. While the vegetables are cooking, coat the fish fillets with the remaining 2 tablespoons of oil and the lime juice. Sprinkle with the remaining 1 teaspoon of curry, and season with salt and pepper. Place the fillets on the sheet pan.

6. When there are 20 minutes remaining, place the sheet pan on the wire rack. Close the oven door and continue cooking for 15 to 20 minutes.

7. Cooking is complete when an instant-read thermometer inserted in the fish reads 145ºF (63ºC). Serve the fish with the vegetables and pineapple.

Salmon with Bok Choy

Prep time: 15 minutes | Cook time: 15 minutes | Serves 8

$^1/_3$ cup pure maple syrup

3 tablespoons soy sauce

3 garlic cloves, minced

8 (6-ounce / 170-g) skinless salmon fillets

1 pound (454 g) baby carrots

8 heads baby bok choy, quartered lengthwise

Canola oil cooking spray

1 bunch scallions, green parts only, thinly sliced, for serving

1.   In a small bowl, stir together the maple syrup, soy sauce, and garlic. Place the salmon fillets in a resealable bag and pour half of the marinade over the salmon, reserving the other half. Seal the bag and marinate in the refrigerator for at least 20 minutes and up to 12 hours.

2.   Once the fish has marinated, nest the roast tray in a sheet pan. Lightly coat the roast tray with cooking spray. Arrange the salmon fillets on the roast tray.

3.   In a large bowl, toss the carrots and bok choy with the reserved marinade. Evenly arrange the vegetables in the air fryer basket.

4.   Install a wire rack on Level 1. Select AIR ROAST, select 2 LEVEL, set the temperature to 400ºF (204ºC), and set the time to 15 minutes. Press START/STOP to begin preheating.

5.   When the unit has preheated, place the sheet pan and roast tray on the wire rack and insert the air fryer basket on Level 4. Close the oven door to begin cooking.

6.   When cooking is complete, top the salmon with the scallions and serve alongside the carrots and bok choy.

Baked Golden Shrimp

Prep time: 15 minutes | Cook time: 20 minutes | Serves 3 to 4

1 pound (454 g) (16- to 20-count) shrimp, peeled and deveined

6 tablespoons (¾ stick) unsalted butter, melted, divided

½ teaspoon Old Bay seasoning

1 tablespoon minced shallot

2 teaspoons chopped fresh parsley, divided

1 teaspoon minced garlic

Kosher salt and freshly ground black pepper, to taste

$^1/_3$ cup panko bread crumbs

¼ cup dry sherry

1 teaspoon minced fresh thyme

1 lemon, halved

1.   In a large bowl, combine the shrimp, 3 tablespoons of melted butter, the Old Bay seasoning, shallot, 1 teaspoon of parsley, the garlic, salt, and pepper. Toss to coat the shrimp evenly.

2.   In the casserole dish, arrange the shrimp so that they overlap about halfway on top of each other with the tails facing down. Pour any liquid from the bowl over shrimp.

3.   In the same large bowl, mix together the remaining 3 tablespoons of melted butter, the panko bread crumbs, sherry, and thyme until well combined.

4.   Sprinkle the panko bread crumb mixture evenly over the shrimp.

5.   Install a wire rack on Level 3. Select BAKE, set the temperature to 350ºF (177ºC), and set the time to 15 minutes. Press START/STOP to begin preheating.

6.   When the unit has preheated, place the casserole dish on the wire rack. Close the oven door to begin cooking.

7.   After 15 minutes, select BROIL, set the temperature to HI, and press START/STOP to begin. Broil the shrimp for 3 to 5 minutes, until the bread crumbs are golden brown.

8.   When cooking is complete, sprinkle the shrimp bake with the remaining 1 teaspoon of parsley and squeeze the lemon juice over the top before serving.

Butter Cracker Stuffed Shrimp

Prep time: 20 minutes | Cook time: 40 minutes | Serves 4 to 6

8 tablespoons (1 stick) unsalted butter

5 garlic cloves, pressed

2 sleeves Ritz butter crackers, crushed

1 cup panko bread crumbs

$^1/_3$ cup freshly squeezed lemon juice

¼ cup vermouth

½ bunch curly parsley, chopped, plus more for garnish

Kosher salt and freshly ground black pepper, to taste

6 ounces (170 g) bay or sea scallops, chopped

1 pound (454 g) (16- to 20-count) shrimp, peeled and deveined

Lemon wedges, for serving

1.   Place the butter and garlic on the sheet pan.

2.   Install a wire rack on Level 2 and place the sheet pan on it. Select REHEAT, set the temperature to 150ºF (66ºC), and set the time to 5 minutes. Close the oven door and press START/STOP to begin. Cook until the butter is melted.

3.   In a large bowl, gently toss the Ritz crumbs, panko bread crumbs, lemon juice, vermouth, and parsley to combine. Carefully tip the melted butter and garlic into the mixture and toss to combine. Taste and season with salt and pepper.

4.   Add the chopped scallops to the crumb mixture and mix until well combined. (Be sure not to taste the stuffing after the scallops are added.)

5.   Spread the stuffing evenly across the sheet pan used to melt the butter. Place the shrimp on top of the stuffing, arranging them however you like. I recommend alternating rows or linking two shrimp together at a time for a more dramatic presentation.

6.   Select AIR ROAST, set the temperature to 350ºF (177ºC), and set the time to 35 minutes. Press START/STOP to begin preheating.

7.   When the unit has preheated, place the sheet pan on the wire rack. Close the door to begin cooking.

8.   Cooking is complete when the shrimp and scallops are cooked through. This may vary depending on the size of the shrimp. Serve with lemon wedges and garnish with a sprinkle of chopped parsley.

Chicken and Seafood Paella

Prep time: 10 minutes | Cook time: 50 minutes | Serves 6 to 8

2 tablespoons extra-virgin olive oil, divided
4 links chorizo sausage (about 12 ounces / 340 g in total), diced
1 pound (454 g) boneless, skinless chicken thighs, cut into 1-inch pieces
1 small yellow onion, diced
1 red bell pepper, seeded and diced
2 tablespoons minced garlic
1 teaspoon paprika
1 teaspoon kosher salt, divided
¾ teaspoon freshly ground black pepper, divided
2 cups short-grain rice
5 cups chicken stock
1 teaspoon saffron threads
½ cup crushed or diced canned tomatoes
½ cup frozen green peas
8 ounces (227 g) (16- to 20-count) shrimp, peeled and deveined
1 pound (454 g) littleneck clams, scrubbed
2 tablespoons chopped fresh flat-leaf parsley
Lemon wedges, for serving

1. Grease the sheet pan with 1 tablespoon of olive oil. Place the chorizo and chicken side by side on the pan.
2. Install a wire rack on Level 3. Select AIR ROAST, set the temperature to 400ºF (204ºC), and set the time to 50 minutes. Press START/STOP to begin preheating.
3. When the unit has preheated, place the sheet pan on the wire rack. Close the door to begin cooking.
4. After 10 minutes, remove the pan and add the onion, bell pepper, garlic, paprika, ½ teaspoon of salt, and 3/8 teaspoon of black pepper to the meat, and toss to coat. Return the pan to the oven to continue cooking.
5. Bake for 10 more minutes, stirring halfway through.
6. After 10 minutes, add the rice to the pan and toss to incorporate. Spread the mixture in an even layer. Return the pan to the oven to continue cooking.
7. Meanwhile, in a large microwafe-safe measuring cup, combine the chicken stock and saffron. Microwave on high for 2 minutes.
8. After the rice has cooked for 10 minutes, remove the pan and gently stir the stock mixture and tomatoes with their juices into the rice mixture until well combined. Carefully return the pan to the oven to continue cooking.
9. After 20 minutes, increase the oven temperature to 425ºF (218ºC) and remove the pan from the oven. Sprinkle the peas over the rice. Nestle the shrimp into the mixture and arrange the clams evenly over the top. If all of the stock has been absorbed, drizzle 2 tablespoons water over the rice (if it seems dry, add 1 more tablespoon water). Drizzle the remaining 1 tablespoon of olive oil over the paella, and sprinkle with the remaining ½ teaspoon salt and remaining 3/8 teaspoon pepper. Carefully return the pan to the oven to continue cooking.
10. Bake until the clams have opened, 6 to 8 minutes. Remove the pan from the oven and garnish the paella with the chopped parsley. Serve with lemon wedges.

Spicy Bacon-Stuffed Gold Clams

Prep time: 10 minutes | Cook time: 40 to 42 minutes | Serves 6 to 8

24 littleneck clams, scrubbed

6 ounces (170 g) bacon, minced

½ cup minced red bell pepper

½ cup minced shallots

½ to ¾ cup Italian bread crumbs, divided

¼ cup grated Parmesan cheese

1 tablespoon chipotle hot sauce

1 teaspoon smoked paprika

½ teaspoon chili powder

½ teaspoon garlic powder

1 teaspoon kosher salt

½ teaspoon freshly ground black pepper

2 tablespoons chopped fresh parsley

Lemon wedges, for serving

1.   Install a wire rack on Level 3. Select AIR ROAST, set the temperature to 400ºF (204ºC), and set the time to 5 minutes. Press START/STOP to begin preheating.

2.   Place the clams on the sheet pan.

3.   When the unit has preheated, place the sheet pan on the wire rack. Close the oven door to begin cooking. Roast the clams for 5 minutes, or until they open.

4.   When cooking is complete, remove the pan from the oven. Discard any clams that have not opened. Remove the meat, reserving the shells. Drain any juice from the clams into a measuring cup, and pour ¼ cup of the liquid into a medium bowl. Mince the clam meat and place it in the bowl with the clam juice.

5.   Put the bacon, bell pepper, and shallots on the same sheet pan. Place the sheet pan on the wire rack and close the oven door.

6.   Select AIR ROAST, set the temperature to 400ºF (204ºC), and set the time to 20 minutes. Press START/STOP to begin cooking.

7.   When cooking is complete, the bacon should be crispy. In a large bowl, toss the mixture with ½ cup of bread crumbs, the Parmesan, hot sauce, paprika, chili powder, garlic powder, salt, pepper, and parsley. Add the clams and juice and toss to combine. If the mixture is very wet, add the remaining bread crumbs 1 tablespoon at a time. Fill each clamshell with about 1 tablespoon of the stuffing and place the shells on the sheet pan. Not all the shells will be used.

8.   Place the sheet pan on the wire rack and close the oven door. Select AIR ROAST, set the temperature to 400ºF (204ºC), and set the time to 17 minutes. Press START/STOP to begin cooking.

9.   Roast the stuffed clams for 15 to 17 minutes. Serve with lemon wedges.

CHAPTER 7: VEGETARIAN SIDES AND MAINS

Squash, Zucchini, and Eggplant Ratatouille

Prep time: 30 minutes | Cook time: 50 minutes | Serves 4

1 (24-ounce / 680-g) jar marinara sauce

2 summer squash

2 zucchini

2 Japanese eggplants

6 Roma tomatoes

4 tablespoons extra-virgin olive oil, divided

1 teaspoon dried herbes de Provence

Kosher salt and freshly ground black pepper, to taste

2 garlic cloves

¼ cup fresh basil leaves

¼ cup fresh parsley leaves

1.   Spread the marinara evenly in the pie plate.

2.   Cut the squash, zucchini, eggplants, and tomatoes into ¼-inch-thick slices. Even slices are key to ensure all the vegetables cook at the same time, so take care.

3.   Taking one slice of summer squash, zucchini, eggplant, and tomato, arrange them concentrically about three-quarters of the way up each other, starting on the outside of the pie plate. Repeat this process with the vegetable slices, shingling them in the same order. When you get to the end of the dish, keep the process going in the opposite direction across the dish. This will give the vegetables a domino-looking affect. Repeat the process until the dish is full.

4.   Drizzle the vegetables with 2 tablespoons of olive oil, and season them with the herbes de Provence, salt, and pepper. Cover the dish with foil.

5.   Install a wire rack on Level 3. Select AIR ROAST, set the temperature to 400ºF (204ºC), and set the time to 50 minutes. Press START/STOP to begin preheating.

6.   When the unit has preheated, place the casserole dish on the wire rack. Close the oven door to begin cooking.

7.   Mince the garlic and chop the basil and parsley. Place them in a small bowl, add the remaining 2 tablespoons of olive oil, and season with salt and pepper. Toss to combine and set aside.

8.   After 40 minutes, remove the dish from the oven and remove the foil. Drizzle the herb mixture over the vegetables. Place the casserole dish back on the wire rack to continue cooking for the remaining 10 minutes.

9.   When cooking is complete, remove the dish from the oven, and serve.

Super Cheesy Eggplant Lasagna

Prep time: 20 minutes | Cook time: 35 minutes | Serves 6 to 8

1 (15-ounce / 425-g) container ricotta cheese

8 ounces (227 g) Parmesan cheese, shredded or grated

1 bunch fresh parsley, chopped

2 (24-ounce / 680-g) jars marinara sauce

2 globe eggplants, cut into discs and lightly salted

16 ounces (454 g) Mozzarella cheese, shredded

1 (16-ounce / 454-g) package frozen Mozzarella sticks

1.   In a large bowl, mix together the ricotta, Parmesan, and parsley until well combined. Set aside.

2.   Spoon a thin layer of marinara sauce across the bottom of the casserole dish.

3.   Place an even layer of the salted eggplant discs on bottom of the dish. Using the back of a spoon, spread a layer of the ricotta mixture on top of the eggplant. Top with more marinara sauce, then sprinkle with some shredded Mozzarella. Repeat until three-quarters of the dish is filled. Cover the dish with foil.

4.   Install a wire rack on Level 1. Select AIR ROAST, set the temperature to 375ºF (191ºC), and set the time to 25 minutes. Press START/STOP to begin preheating.

5.   When the unit has preheated, place the casserole dish on the wire rack. Close the oven door to begin cooking.

6.   When cooking is complete, remove the dish from the oven and remove the foil. Arrange the frozen Mozzarella sticks evenly on top.

7.   Select AIR ROAST, set the temperature to 375ºF (191ºC), and set the time to 10 minutes. Press START/STOP to begin preheating.

8.   When the unit has preheated, place the casserole dish on the wire rack. Close the oven door to begin cooking.

9.   When cooking is complete, remove the dish from the oven. Let the lasagna cool for 5 to 10 minutes before serving.

Roasted Mushroom Enchiladas

Prep time: 10 minutes | Cook time: 35 minutes | Serves 8 to 12

8 ounces (227 g) white mushrooms, sliced
2 poblano peppers, seeded and diced
2 ears corn, shucked and kernels cut from cobs
1 medium white onion, diced
¼ cup canola oil
1 teaspoon chili powder
1 teaspoon garlic powder
1 teaspoon ground cumin
1 teaspoon smoked paprika
2 tablespoons freshly squeezed lime juice
2 cups shredded Mozzarella cheese, divided
Kosher salt and freshly ground black pepper, to taste
2 (10-ounce / 283-g) cans green enchilada sauce, divided
6 to 8 fajita-size flour tortillas
Chopped fresh cilantro, for garnish
Lime wedges, for serving

1. In a large bowl, toss together the mushrooms, peppers, corn kernels, onion, canola oil, chili powder, garlic powder, cumin, and paprika until the vegetables are well coated. Arrange the vegetables on the sheet pan in a single layer.
2. Install a wire rack on Level 3. Select AIR ROAST, set the temperature to 400ºF (204ºC), and set the time to 20 minutes. Press START/STOP to begin preheating.
3. When the unit has preheated, place the sheet pan on the wire rack. Close the oven door to begin cooking.
4. When cooking is complete, remove the pan from the oven and let the vegetables cool.
5. Drain off any liquid from the pan. Transfer the roasted vegetables to a large bowl and add the lime juice and 1 cup of Mozzarella. Season with salt and pepper and stir to combine.
6. Pour 1 can of enchilada sauce in the bottom of the casserole dish.
7. Lay out the tortillas and place up to ¼ cup of filling in the center of each. Roll up the tortillas and place them seam-side down in the dish. Pour the remaining 1 can of enchilada sauce over the enchiladas and top with the remaining 1 cup of Mozzarella. Cover with foil.
8. Select AIR ROAST, set the temperature to 400ºF (204ºC), and set the time to 15 minutes. Press START/STOP to begin preheating.
9. When the unit has preheated, place the sheet pan on the wire rack. Close the oven door to begin cooking.
10. When there are 5 minutes remaining, remove the foil and continue to cook to brown the top.
11. When cooking is complete, remove the pan from the oven and garnish with the cilantro. Serve with lime wedges.

Coconut Tofu, Chickpea, and Kale Curry

Prep time: 20 minutes | Cook time: 25 minutes | Serves 6 to 8

2 tablespoons soy sauce

1 tablespoon maple syrup

2 tablespoons curry powder

1 pound (454 g) firm tofu, cut into 1-inch cubes

¼ cup unsweetened shredded coconut

1 head cauliflower, cut into 1-inch florets

1 (15-ounce / 425-g) can chickpeas, drained and rinsed

1 bunch (about 12 ounces / 340 g) kale, stemmed and chopped

1 (13-ounce / 369-g) can coconut cream

Canola oil cooking spray

1.   In a bowl, combine the soy sauce, maple syrup, and curry powder. Place the tofu cubes in a resealable bag and pour in the marinade. Seal the bag and let the tofu marinate for 30 minutes at room temperature.

2.   Put the coconut in a medium bowl. Remove the tofu cubes from the bag, reserving the marinade, and dredge the tofu in the coconut.

3.   Put the cauliflower, chickpeas, and kale in large bowl. Add the reserved marinade and the coconut cream. Stir until well mixed.

4.   Lightly coat the air fryer basket with cooking spray. Evenly arrange the coconut-coated tofu cubes in the basket. Using a slotted spoon, transfer the cauliflower mixture to the sheet pan, reserving the excess coconut sauce.

5.   Install a wire rack on Level 1. Select AIR FRY, select 2 LEVEL, set the temperature to 400ºF (204ºC), and set the time to 25 minutes. Press START/STOP to begin prehearing.

6.   When the unit has preheated, place the sheet pan on the wire rack and insert the air fryer basket on Level 4. Close the oven door to begin cooking.

7.   When cooking is complete, transfer the tofu to a serving dish. Top with the cauliflower mixture and drizzle with the reserved coconut sauce. Serve immediately.

Spaghetti Squash with Parmesan Mushroom

Prep time: 15 minutes | Cook time: 45 minutes | Serves 4 to 6

1 spaghetti squash, halved lengthwise and seeded

Extra-virgin olive oil, for brushing the squash

1 teaspoon garlic salt

1 teaspoon paprika

¼ teaspoon freshly ground black pepper, plus more to taste

½ teaspoon kosher salt, plus more to taste

6 small portabella mushrooms, stemmed

1 cup all-purpose flour

3 large eggs, beaten

2 cups bread crumbs

Cooking oil spray

1½ cups jarred spaghetti sauce

2 cups shredded Mozzarella cheese

1. Line the sheet pan with parchment paper. Place the spaghetti squash halves cut-side up on the pan and brush the flesh with olive oil.

2. Install a wire rack on Level 1. Select AIR FRY, set the temperature to 400ºF (204ºC), and set the time to 45 minutes. Press START/STOP to begin preheating.

3. When the unit has preheated, place the sheet pan on the wire rack. Close the oven door to begin cooking.

4. Meanwhile, clean the mushrooms by wiping them with a wet cloth. Use a spoon to scoop out and discard the gills.

5. Set up your breading station: Line up three shallow bowls. Put the flour in one bowl, the eggs in the second, and the bread crumbs in the third. One at a time, coat the mushroom caps in flour, then dip them in the eggs, and finally, coat them in the bread crumbs. Place the mushrooms in the air fryer basket in a single layer. Spray them all over with cooking spray to promote even browning during cooking.

6. After the squash has cooked for 25 minutes, insert the air fryer basket on Level 3.

7. When there are 5 minutes remaining, remove the basket and spoon a bit of spaghetti sauce on each mushroom cap, then sprinkle with the Mozzarella. Return the basket to the oven to continue cooking for the remaining 5 minutes.

8. When cooking is complete, remove the spaghetti squash from the oven and carefully use a fork to remove the flesh from the rind. It will pull apart like spaghetti strands. Season the squash with salt and pepper and serve with the browned portabella Parmesan.

Classic Succotash

Prep time: 15 minutes | Cook time: 20 minutes | Serves 4 to 6

Cooking oil spray

10 cups fresh corn kernels (from about 12 ears)

2½ cups cherry tomatoes, halved

8 garlic cloves, minced

2 small onions, chopped

2 cups frozen lima beans

8 tablespoons (1 stick) unsalted butter, cut into small cubes

Kosher salt and freshly ground black pepper, to taste

Thinly sliced fresh basil, for garnish

1.   Lightly coat the sheet pans with cooking spray.

2.   Divide the corn, cherry tomatoes, garlic, onions, lima beans, and butter cubes between the two pans. Season with salt and pepper and thoroughly mix to combine.

3.   Install the wire racks on Levels 1 and 3. Select AIR ROAST, select 2 LEVEL, set the temperature to 350ºF (177ºC), and set the time to 20 minutes. Press START/STOP to begin preheating.

4.   When the unit has preheated, place a sheet pan on each wire rack. Close the oven door to begin cooking.

5.   After 10 minutes, open the oven and stir the vegetables. Close the oven door to continue cooking.

6.   When cooking is complete, garnish the succotash with the basil and serve.

Mac and Cheese

Prep time: 15 minutes | Cook time: 1 hour | Serves 8

1 cup cottage cheese

2 cups whole milk

1 teaspoon Dijon mustard

½ teaspoon dry mustard

¼ teaspoon garlic powder

¼ teaspoon onion powder

Pinch ground cayenne pepper

Kosher salt and freshly ground black pepper, to taste

1 pound (454 g) elbow macaroni

8 ounces (227 g) sharp Cheddar cheese, shredded

8 ounces (227 g) Mozzarella cheese, shredded, divided

½ cup grated Parmesan cheese

Cooking oil spray

½ cup panko bread crumbs

2 tablespoons unsalted butter, melted

1.   In a blender or food processor, combine the cottage cheese, milk, Dijon and dry mustards, garlic powder, onion powder, cayenne, salt, and pepper. Blend until smooth.

2.   In a large bowl, combine the cottage cheese mixture, elbow macaroni, Cheddar, half of the Mozzarella, and the Parmesan until well mixed.

3.   Coat the casserole dish with cooking spray. Arrange the pasta mixture in the dish. Cover tightly with foil.

4.   Install a wire rack on Level 4. Select BAKE, set the temperature to 375ºF (191ºC), and set the time to 60 minutes. Press START/STOP to begin preheating.

5.   When the unit has preheated, place the casserole dish on the wire rack. Close the oven door to begin cooking.

6.   Meanwhile, in a small bowl, combine the panko with the melted butter and the remaining half of the Mozzarella.

7.   After 30 minutes, remove the casserole dish from the oven and remove the foil. Stir gently and spread the bread crumb mixture evenly on top.

8.   Return the casserole dish to the oven and continue cooking for the remaining 30 minutes, or until golden brown.

9.   When cooking is complete, let the macaroni and cheese cool for 10 minutes before serving.

Corn Bread

Prep time: 10 minutes | Cook time: 40 minutes | Serves 8

3 cups whole milk

½ cup canola oil, plus more for greasing

3 large eggs

¼ cup dark molasses

2¼ cups all-purpose flour

2¼ cups cornmeal

$^1/_3$ cup sugar

1 tablespoon baking powder

1 cup shredded sharp Cheddar cheese

1 teaspoon kosher salt

1.   In a large bowl, whisk together the milk, oil, eggs, and molasses until smooth and well incorporated.

2.   Add the flour, cornmeal, sugar, baking powder, Cheddar, and salt to the bowl and whisk well to combine. There should be no clumps of dry ingredients in the mixture.

3.   Grease the casserole dish with canola oil. Pour the corn bread batter into the dish.

4.   Install a wire rack on Level 3. Select BAKE, set the temperature to 315ºF (157ºC), and set the time to 40 minutes. Press START/STOP to begin preheating.

5.   When the unit has preheated, place the casserole dish on the wire rack. Close the oven door to begin cooking.

6.   When cooking is complete, let the corn bread cool for 5 minutes before removing it from the dish and serving.

Gnocchi with Roasted Zucchini and Peppers

Prep time: 10 minutes | Cook time: 20 minutes | Serves 4 to 6

Cooking oil spray

1 pound (454 g) potato gnocchi, boiled and drained

1 pint cherry tomatoes

1 small zucchini, halved lengthwise and cut into ¼-inch-thick half moons

1 red bell pepper, seeded and cut into thin strips

1 yellow bell pepper, seeded and cut into thin strips

1 red onion, sliced

1 cup basil pesto

¼ cup grated Parmesan cheese

Fresh basil leaves, for garnish

1.   Coat the sheet pan with cooking spray and set aside.

2.   In a large bowl, combine the gnocchi, tomatoes, zucchini, bell peppers, and onion with the pesto until evenly coated. Divide the mixture between the two pans and spread in an even layer.

3.   Install the wire racks on Levels 1 and 3. Select BAKE, select 2 LEVEL, set the temperature to 425ºF (218ºC), and set the time to 20 minutes. Press START/STOP to begin preheating.

4.   When the unit has preheated, place a sheet pan on each wire rack. Close the oven door to begin cooking.

5.   After 10 minutes, remove the sheet pans and use tongs to toss the mixture. Spread the mixture into an even layer and return the sheet pan to the oven. Close the oven door to continue cooking for the remaining 10 minutes.

6.   When cooking is completed, sprinkle with the Parmesan and garnish with the basil leaves. Serve immediately.

CHAPTER 8: ENTERTAINING

Candied Pecans, Walnuts, and Almonds

Prep time: 5 minutes | Cook time: 23 minutes | Serves 6 to 8

1 cup pecans

1 cup walnuts

1 cup almonds

¼ cup maple syrup

¼ cup granulated sugar

2 tablespoons light brown sugar

¼ teaspoon cayenne pepper

1 tablespoon dried herbes de Provence

1 teaspoon kosher salt

1.   In a large bowl, mix together the pecans, walnuts, almonds, maple syrup, granulated sugar, brown sugar, cayenne pepper, herbes de Provence, and salt until well combined and the nuts are coated.

2.   Line the sheet pan with parchment paper. Pour the nuts onto the pan and spread them into an even layer.

3.   Install a wire rack on Level 3. Select AIR ROAST, set the temperature to 350ºF (177ºC), and set the time to 23 minutes. Press START/STOP to begin preheating.

4.   When the unit has preheated, place the sheet pan on the wire rack. Close the oven door to begin cooking.

5.   Every 8 minutes through the cooking time, open the oven door and stir the nuts. When cooking is complete, remove the nuts from the oven and let cool completely.

Lush Snack Mix

Prep time: 10 minutes | Cook time: 45 minutes | Serves 16

3 cups whole-wheat cereal

3 cups corn cereal

3 cups rice cereal

1 cup pretzel sticks

1 cup bagel chips

1 cup lightly salted roasted peanuts

1 cup cheese crackers

8 tablespoons (1 stick) unsalted butter, melted

3 tablespoons Worcestershire sauce

2 teaspoons seasoned salt

1 teaspoon garlic powder

1.   In a large bowl, combine the whole-wheat cereal, corn cereal, rice cereal, pretzel sticks, bagel chips, peanuts, and cheese crackers.

2.   In a small bowl, mix together the melted butter, Worcestershire sauce, salt, and garlic powder. Pour the mixture over the dry ingredients and mix until they are thoroughly coated.

3.   Divide the mixture between the two sheet pans, spreading it into an even layer.

4.   Install the wire racks on Levels 1 and 3. Select BAKE, set the temperature to 315ºF (157ºC), and set the time to 45 minutes. Press START/STOP to begin preheating.

5.   When the unit has preheated, place the sheet pans on the wire racks. Close the oven door to begin cooking.

6.   When there are 23 minutes remaining, remove the pans from the oven and place on trivets or a wooden cutting board. Stir the contents of each pan and spread each back into an even layer. Return the pans to the oven and continue cooking for the remaining 23 minutes, or until the party mix is slightly toasted and fragrant.

7.   When cooking is complete, remove the pans from the oven and let the mix cool completely.

Cauliflower and Asparagus Pita Platter

Prep time: 20 minutes | Cook time: 20 minutes | Serves 8

1 head cauliflower, cut into 1-inch florets

1 bunch asparagus, woody ends trimmed

5 baby bell peppers, halved and seeded

1 tablespoon curry powder

1 tablespoon canola oil

Kosher salt and freshly ground black pepper, to taste

1 (5-ounce / 142-g) block feta cheese

5 pitas, quartered

1 (8-ounce / 227-g) can Greek dolmas (stuffed grape leaves)

1 (6-ounce / 170-g) jar olive tapenade

Chopped fresh parsley, for garnish

1.   In a large bowl, combine the cauliflower, asparagus, bell peppers, curry powder, canola oil, salt, and black pepper. Toss to coat the vegetables. Arrange the mixture in the air fryer basket.

2.   Place the block of feta on the sheet pan.

3.   Install a wire rack on Level 1. Select AIR FRY, select 2 LEVEL, set the temperature to 400ºF (204ºC), and set the time to 20 minutes. Press START/STOP to begin preheating.

4.   When the unit has preheated, place the sheet pan on the wire rack and insert the air fryer basket on Level 3.

5.   After 10 minutes, remove the sheet pan and add the pita quarters to it. Remove the basket and move the wire rack to Level 3. Insert the air fryer basket on Level 1 and place the sheet pan on the wire rack. Close the oven door to continue cooking.

6.   When cooking is complete, the feta should be brown and the inside soft and spreadable. Place the feta on a platter and top with the tapenade. Arrange the warm vegetables, dolmas, and pitas around it. Garnish the vegetables with parsley before serving.

Crostini with Crab BLT Dip

Prep time: 10 minutes | Cook time: 20 minutes | Serves 6 to 8

1 pound (454 g) lump crabmeat

1 pound (454 g) whipped cream cheese

1 cup mayonnaise

½ teaspoon onion powder

½ teaspoon smoked paprika

1 cup thinly sliced scallions, white and green parts

2 cups shredded Monterey Jack cheese, divided

2 tablespoons canola oil

1 loaf French bread, thinly sliced

10 bacon slices, cooked until crisp, crumbled (about 1 cup)

1 cup shredded iceberg lettuce

1 cup diced tomatoes

1.   In a large bowl, mix together the crabmeat, cream cheese, mayonnaise, onion powder, paprika, scallions, and 1 cup of shredded cheese until well combined. Evenly spread the mixture on the bottom of the casserole dish. Top with the remaining 1 cup of cheese.

2.   Lightly brush the oil on one side of the bread slices. Arrange the bread in a single layer on the sheet pan, oil-side up.

3.   Install the wire racks on Level 1 and 3. Select BAKE, select 2 LEVEL, set the temperature to 375ºF (191ºC), and set the time to 20 minutes. Press START/STOP to begin preheating.

4.   When the unit has preheated, place the casserole dish on the Level 1 wire rack and the sheet pan on the Level 3 wire rack. Close the oven door to begin cooking.

5.   After 10 minutes, remove the sheet pan. Close the oven door and continue cooking the dip.

6.   When cooking is complete, top the dip with the crumbled bacon, lettuce, and tomatoes. Serve alongside the toasted bread. Serve immediately.

Pull-Apart Cranberry Bread

Prep time: 10 minutes | Cook time: 20 minutes | Serves 16

1 (20-ounce / 567-g) loaf oval sourdough bread

12 tablespoons (1½ sticks) butter, melted

2 tablespoons minced fresh rosemary

2 tablespoons minced fresh parsley

2 tablespoons minced garlic

2 (15-ounce / 425-g) can whole-berry cranberry sauce

2 (8-ounce / 227-g) wheel Brie cheese, cut into ¼-inch slices

½ cup shredded Parmesan cheese

1.   Using a serrated knife, cut a 1-inch square grid pattern into the loaf, leaving the bottom ½ inch of the loaf uncut. Put it on a sheet of foil.

2.   In a small bowl, mix together the melted butter, rosemary, parsley, and garlic. Using a silicone brush, brush the bread with the butter mixture, making sure to get in between every piece.

3.   Stuff the buttered bread with the cranberry sauce and Brie slices and sprinkle with the Parmesan. Loosely wrap the bread in foil. Place it on the sheet pan.

4.   Install a wire rack on Level 4. Select WHOLE ROAST, set the temperature to 350ºF (177ºC), and set the time to 20 minutes. Press START/STOP to begin preheating.

5.   When the unit has preheated, place the sheet pan on the wire rack. Close the oven door to begin cooking.

6.   After 10 minutes, remove the pan from the oven and remove the foil. Return the sheet pan to the oven and continue cooking for the remaining 10 minutes.

7.   When cooking is complete, the cheese should be melty and the bread toasted and golden brown. Serve warm.

Honey Ham with Orange Carrots

Prep time: 20 minutes | Cook time: 1 hour 20 minutes | Serves 8

1 (7- to 10-pound / 3.2- to 4.5-kg) spiral-cut ham with glaze packet

3 tablespoons freshly squeezed orange juice

½ teaspoon ground cayenne pepper

¼ teaspoon ground ginger

1 teaspoon kosher salt

2 (12-ounce / 340-g) bags baby carrots

2 tablespoons Dijon mustard

2 tablespoons whole-grain mustard

¼ cup water

1.   Install a wire rack on Level 1. Select AIR ROAST, set the temperature to 325ºF (163ºC), and set the time to 1 hour 20 minutes. Press START/STOP to begin preheating.

2.   Remove the ham from its packaging (set the glaze packet aside) and place the ham sliced-side up in the casserole dish.

3.   When the unit has preheated, place the casserole dish on the wire rack. Close the oven door to begin cooking.

4.   Meanwhile, in a medium bowl, combine the contents of the glaze packet with the orange juice and whisk until combined. Remove ½ cup of the glaze and set aside. Add the cayenne, ginger, and salt to the glaze in the bowl and stir to combine. Add the carrots and toss to coat in the glaze.

5.   When there are 50 minutes remaining, remove the dish from the oven. Arrange the carrots on the pan around the ham. Place the casserole dish back on the wire rack and continue cooking.

6.   To the reserved glaze, whisk in the Dijon mustard, whole-grain mustard, and water.

7.   When there are 30 minutes remaining, remove the ham from the oven and drizzle the mustard glaze over the top, making sure to get in between the slices.

8.   Reduce the oven temperature to 300ºF (149ºC), place the ham back in the oven, and continue cooking for the remaining time.

9.   When cooking is complete, remove the ham from the oven and let cool for 5 to 10 minutes. Use a slotted spoon to remove the carrots from the dish. Slice the ham and serve it along with the carrots.

Italian Parmesan Meatball al Forno

Prep time: 20 minutes | Cook time: 35 minutes | Serves 6 to 8

½ cup Italian-style bread crumbs

¼ cup whole milk

2 pounds (907 g) ground meatloaf mix (ground beef, pork, and veal)

1½ cups grated Parmesan cheese, divided

2 large eggs, beaten

1 teaspoon garlic powder

1 teaspoon red pepper flakes

1 tablespoon Italian seasoning

Kosher salt and freshly ground black pepper, to taste

1 (24-ounce / 680-g) jar marinara sauce

½ cup beef stock

8 ounces (227 g) Mozzarella cheese

Fresh basil leaves, torn, for garnish

1. In a large bowl, stir together the bread crumbs and milk and let sit for 5 minutes.
2. After the bread crumbs and milk have sat for 5 minutes, add the meatloaf mix, ¾ cup of Parmesan, the eggs, garlic powder, red pepper flakes, Italian seasoning, salt, and pepper to the bowl. Mix well to thoroughly combine.
3. Using a ¼-cup measure, fill it with the meatloaf mixture, then roll it into balls. Place the meatballs on the roast tray nested in a sheet pan.
4. Install a wire rack on Level 3. Select AIR ROAST, set the temperature to 400ºF (204ºC), and set the time to 30 minutes. Press START/STOP to begin preheating.
5. When the unit has preheated, place the sheet pan and roast tray on the wire rack. Close the oven door to begin cooking.
6. Meanwhile, combine the marinara sauce and beef stock in the casserole dish.
7. After 15 minutes, remove the sheet pan and roast tray from the oven and place the meatballs, browned-side down, in the sauce in the casserole dish. Place the casserole dish on the wire rack and continue cooking.
8. When cooking is complete, remove the dish and sprinkle the meatballs with the Mozzarella and remaining ½ cup of Parmesan.
9. Select BROIL, set the temperature to HI, and set the time to 5 minutes. Press START/STOP to begin.
10. Place the casserole dish on the wire rack and broil until the cheese is melted and starting to brown. Garnish with the basil before serving.

Parmesan Beef Roast

Prep time: 15 minutes | Cook time: 55 minutes | Serves 8

1 (4-pound / 1.8-kg) beef roast (whole tenderloin or sirloin roast)

8 tablespoons (½ cup) canola oil, divided

Kosher salt and freshly ground black pepper, to taste

3 pounds (1.4 kg) fingerling or baby red potatoes, halved

8 bacon slices, cut into ½-inch pieces

1 cup grated Parmesan cheese

1 cup plain bread crumbs

¼ cup chopped fresh parsley

2 tablespoons chopped fresh rosemary

1.　　Place the beef roast on the roast tray nested in a sheet pan. Pour 2 tablespoons of canola oil on the roast and rub it evenly all over the meat. Season the beef with salt and pepper.

2.　　Install a wire rack on Level 1. Select AIR ROAST, set the temperature to 400ºF (204ºC), and set the time to 55 minutes. Press START/STOP to begin preheating.

3.　　When the unit has preheated, place the sheet pan and roast tray on the wire rack. Close the oven door to begin cooking.

4.　　Meanwhile, in a large bowl, combine the potatoes, bacon, 2 tablespoons of canola oil, salt, and pepper. Mix well to coat the potatoes.

5.　　In a medium bowl, combine the Parmesan, bread crumbs, remaining 4 tablespoons of canola oil, the parsley, rosemary, salt, and pepper. Mix well to combine.

6.　　When there are 35 minutes remaining, remove the sheet pan and roast tray from the oven. Carefully pack the bread crumb mixture on the top and sides of the beef. Transfer the potatoes to the air fryer basket.

7.　　Place the sheet pan and roast tray back on the wire rack, and insert the air fryer basket on Level 3. Set the temperature to 360ºF (182ºC), and close the oven door to continue cooking.

8.　　When cooking is complete, remove the beef from the oven and let it rest for up to 10 minutes. Leave the potatoes in the oven to stay warm while the beef rests. After 10 minutes, slice the beef and serve with the potatoes.

Beef, Clam, and Veggie Hot Dish

Prep time: 15 minutes | Cook time: 55 minutes | Serves 20

4 pounds (1.8 kg) 90% lean ground beef, divided

2 teaspoons onion powder, divided

2 teaspoons garlic powder, divided

Kosher salt and freshly ground black pepper, to taste

2 (16-ounce / 454-g) cans Boston baked beans, divided

2 (16-ounce / 454-g) bags frozen mixed vegetables, divided

2 (28-ounce / 794-g) cans New England clam chowder, divided

2 pounds (907 g) frozen tater tots, divided

2 (12-ounce / 340-g) packages frozen clam strips, divided

1.   Place 2 pounds (907 g) of ground beef in each casserole dish and press into an even layer to cover the bottom of the dish. Season the meat in each dish with 1 teaspoon of onion powder, 1 teaspoon of garlic powder, salt, and pepper.

2.   Install the wire racks on Levels 1 and 3. Select AIR ROAST, select 2 LEVEL, set the temperature to 375ºF (191ºC), and set the time to 55 minutes. Press START/STOP to begin preheating.

3.   When the unit has preheated, place a casserole dish on each wire rack. Close the oven door to begin cooking.

4.   When there are 40 minutes remaining, remove the casserole dishes from the oven.

5.   Evenly pour 1 can of baked beans over the top of the ground beef in one casserole dish. In a medium bowl, stir 1 bag of frozen vegetables together with 1 can of clam chowder, then use a spatula to spread the mixture evenly over the baked beans. Place 1 pound (454 g) of tater tots and 1 package of clam strips on top of the vegetables, ensuring they are evenly spread out. Repeat for the other casserole.

6.   Place the casserole dishes back on the wire racks and close the oven door to resume cooking.

7.   When cooking is complete, remove the casserole dishes from the oven and serve.

Lamb Leg and Vegetable Medley

Prep time: 20 minutes | Cook time: 1 hour | Serves 8 to 10

12 garlic cloves

3 tablespoons fresh rosemary

¼ cup chicken stock, plus more as needed

4 tablespoons (½ stick) unsalted butter, melted

2 teaspoons kosher salt, divided

2 teaspoons freshly ground black pepper, divided

1 (3-pound / 1.4-kg) bone-in leg of lamb

2 tablespoons canola oil

3 carrots, cut into 1-inch pieces

2 medium yellow onions, cut into 1-inch pieces

8 ounces (227 g) Brussels sprouts, stems trimmed, halved lengthwise

1.   In a blender or food processor, combine the garlic, rosemary, chicken stock, melted butter, 1 teaspoon of salt, and 1 teaspoon of pepper. Blend until a paste forms. If it is too thick, add a little more stock.

2.   Place the lamb on a cutting board and season with the garlic mixture. Refrigerate the lamb for 1 hour to marinate.

3.   Meanwhile, in a large bowl, drizzle the canola oil over the carrots, onions, and Brussels sprouts and season with the remaining 1 teaspoon salt and 1 teaspoon of pepper. Toss to coat the vegetables. Place the vegetables in the air fryer basket in a single layer.

4.   Once the lamb has marinated, install a wire rack on Level 1. Select WHOLE ROAST, select 2 LEVEL, set the temperature to 400ºF (204ºC), and set the time to 60 minutes. Press START/STOP to begin preheating.

5.   When the unit has preheated, place the lamb on the roast tray nested into a sheet pan and place on the wire rack. Insert the air fryer basket on Level 4. Close the oven door to begin cooking.

6.   Cooking is complete when an instant-read thermometer inserted into the lamb reads 130ºF (54ºC) to 140ºF (60ºC) (for medium-rare). Remove the lamb and vegetables from the oven. Let the lamb rest at least 10 minutes before slicing and serving alongside the roasted vegetables.

Quinoa and Potato Stuffed Turkey

Prep time: 20 minutes | Cook time: 1 hour 20 minutes | Serves6 to 8

2 tablespoons kosher salt

1 tablespoon sugar

1 teaspoon dried sage, divided

1 (5-pound / 2.3-kg) turkey breast

2 cups cooked quinoa

2 cups cubed peeled sweet potatoes (1-inch cubes)

½ cup dried cranberries

3 cups chicken stock

1 tablespoon chopped fresh rosemary

1 tablespoon chopped fresh thyme

1.   In small bowl, combine the salt, sugar, and 1 teaspoon of sage. Rub this all over the turkey breast, then place the turkey in a resealable bag. Refrigerate for 3 days, flipping over the bag once a day.

2.   When ready to cook, remove the turkey from the bag and pat it dry with paper towels. Place the turkey on the roast tray and nest the roast tray in the sheet pan. Let the turkey sit at room temperature while you prepare the stuffing.

3.   In a casserole dish, combine the quinoa, sweet potatoes, cranberries, chicken stock, rosemary, and thyme. Stir well and cover the dish with foil.

4.   Install a wire rack on Level 1. Select WHOLE ROAST, set the temperature to 425ºF (218ºC), and set the time to 20 minutes. Press START/STOP to begin preheating.

5.   When the unit has preheated, place the sheet pan with the turkey on the wire rack. Close the oven door to begin cooking.

6.   After 20 minutes, install another wire rack on Level 3 and place the casserole dish on it. Close the oven door. Select WHOLE ROAST, select 2 LEVEL, set the temperature to 375ºF (191ºC), and set the time to 60 minutes. Press START/STOP to begin cooking.

7.   When cooking is complete, remove the turkey and quinoa stuffing. Uncover the quinoa and fluff it with a fork. An instant-read thermometer inserted into the turkey should read 165ºF (74ºC). Loosely cover the turkey with foil and let it rest for about 10 minutes. Slice and serve alongside the stuffing.

Sumptuous Seafood Newburg Casserole

Prep time: 10 minutes | Cook time: 40 minutes | Serves 6 to 8

2 cups heavy cream

1 (8-ounce / 227-g) package cream cheese, at room temperature

¼ cup dry sherry

2 teaspoons smoked paprika

2 (8-ounce / 227-g) containers lump crabmeat

1 pound (454 g) sea scallops

1 pound (454 g) shrimp, peeled and deveined

8 ounces (227 g) whitefish fillets, such as cod, cut into 2-inch pieces

Kosher salt, to taste

4 large egg yolks

Juice of 1 lemon

5 English muffins, torn into 2-inch pieces

1. In a large bowl, whisk together the cream, cream cheese, sherry, and paprika until smooth.

2. Add the crabmeat, scallops, shrimp, and fish, and season with salt. Mix well to combine. Pour the mixture into the casserole dish.

3. Install a wire rack on Level 3. Select BAKE, set the temperature to 360ºF (182ºC), and set the time to 40 minutes. Press START/STOP to begin preheating.

4. When the unit has preheated, place the casserole dish on the wire rack. Close the oven door to begin cooking.

5. When there are 15 minutes remaining, remove the casserole dish from the oven. Stir the egg yolks and lemon juice into the casserole. Place the English muffin pieces on top, pushing down lightly to partially submerge the bread.

6. Return the casserole dish to the wire rack. Close the oven door to continue cooking.

7. When cooking is complete, let the casserole cool for 5 minutes before serving.

Corn Bread, Pear, and Sausage Casserole

Prep time: 20 minutes | Cook time: 45 minutes | Serves 10 to 15

Unsalted butter, at room temperature, for greasing

2½ pounds (1.1 kg) prepared corn bread, cut into 1-inch cubes (about 13 cups)

1 medium yellow onion, diced

4 celery stalks, cut into ½-inch pieces

2 green pears, cored and cut into ½-inch pieces

1½ pounds (680 g) precooked ground Italian sausage

6 garlic cloves, minced

2 tablespoons dried sage

2 large eggs, beaten

2 cups chicken broth, plus more as needed

Chopped fresh parsley, for garnish

1.   Grease the casserole dish with butter and set aside.

2.   In a large bowl, mix together the corn bread, onion, celery, pears, sausage, garlic, sage, eggs, and chicken broth until well incorporated. If the corn bread mixture feels very dry to the touch, slowly add more chicken broth until it feels slightly wet. Transfer the corn bread mixture to the prepared casserole dish.

3.   Install a wire rack on Level 3. Select BAKE, set the temperature to 350ºF (177ºC), and set the time to 45 minutes. Press START/STOP to begin preheating.

4.   When the unit has preheated, place the casserole dish on the wire rack. Close the oven door to begin cooking.

5.   When cooking is complete, the top of the corn bread will be golden brown. Remove the dish from the oven and let the stuffing cool for 10 minutes. Garnish with parsley and serve.

Dill and Honey Butter Roasted Carrots

Prep time: 10 minutes | Cook time: 20 minutes | Serves 4 to 6

4 tablespoons (½ stick) unsalted butter, at room temperature

3 tablespoons chopped fresh dill

2 tablespoons honey

Kosher salt and freshly ground black pepper, to taste

2 pounds (907 g) carrots, halved lengthwise

2 teaspoons canola oil

1.   In a small bowl, mix together the butter, dill, honey, salt, and pepper.

2.   In a large bowl, toss the carrots with the oil. Place the carrots on the sheet pan in an even layer.

3.   Install a wire rack on Level 3. Select AIR ROAST, set the temperature to 400ºF (204ºC), and set the time to 20 minutes. Press START/STOP to begin preheating.

4.   When the unit has preheated, place the sheet pan on the wire rack. Close the oven door to begin cooking.

5.   After 10 minutes, open the oven and stir the carrots. Close the oven door to resume cooking.

6.   When cooking is complete, remove the carrots from the oven, immediately toss them with the honey-dill butter, and serve.

Basil Heirloom Tomato and Pepper Pie

Prep time: 10 minutes | Cook time: 20 minutes | Serves 4 to 6

4 large ripe heirloom tomatoes

4 tablespoons extra-virgin olive oil, divided

2 roasted red peppers, seeded and sliced

10 fresh basil leaves

Kosher salt and freshly ground black pepper, to taste

3 tablespoons balsamic vinegar, divided

¼ cup panko bread crumbs

¼ cup grated Parmesan cheese

1.   Slice the tomatoes ¼ to ½ inch thick. Set aside.

2.   Drizzle 1 tablespoon of olive oil in the bottom of the baking pan.

3.   Place an even layer of tomatoes—about one-third of the slices—on the bottom of the pan. Make sure the whole bottom is covered; overlapping is fine. Place half of the roasted red pepper slices over the tomatoes and top with a layer of 5 basil leaves. Season with salt and pepper and drizzle with 1 tablespoon of olive oil and 1 tablespoon of balsamic vinegar. Repeat with another layer of tomatoes, roasted red pepper, basil, salt, pepper, balsamic vinegar, and olive oil. Top the pie with the remaining one-third of tomato slices and remaining olive oil and balsamic vinegar. Drizzle with the remaining 1 tablespoon of vinegar and sprinkle the panko bread crumbs and Parmesan on top.

4.   Install a wire rack on Level 3. Select AIR ROAST, set the temperature to 450ºF (232ºC), and set the time to 20 minutes. Press START/STOP to begin preheating.

5.   When the unit has preheated, place the sheet pan on the wire rack. Close the oven door to begin cooking.

6.   When cooking is complete, remove the tomato pie from the oven. Serve warm or cooled.

Simple Roasted Baby Potatoes

Prep time: 10 minutes | Cook time: 35 minutes | Serves 6

2 pounds (907 g) baby potatoes

2 cups kosher salt

1.   Cut the potatoes in half or in quarters so that each piece is no bigger than 1½ inches.

2.   Cover the bottom of the sheet pan with the salt in an even layer. Arrange the potatoes in an even layer on top of the salt.

3.   Install a wire rack on Level 2. Select AIR ROAST, set the temperature to 450ºF (232ºC), and set the time to 35 minutes. Press START/STOP to begin preheating.

4.   When the unit has preheated, place the sheet pan on the wire rack. Close the door to begin cooking.

5.   When cooking is complete, remove the sheet pan from the oven and check for doneness. Cooking is complete when the potatoes are brown and crispy outside and soft and creamy inside.

Prep time: 30 minutes | Cook time: 16 minutes | Serves 4

Cooking oil spray

1 (16.3-ounce / 462-g) tube large biscuits (8 biscuits)

12 ounces (340 g) frozen cranberries

½ cup granulated sugar

$^1/_3$ cup fresh orange juice

2 tablespoons cornstarch

1½ pounds (680 g) (about 2 medium) sweet potatoes, peeled and chopped

¾ cup whole milk, divided

2 tablespoons unsalted butter, at room temperature

2 tablespoons light brown sugar

½ teaspoon vanilla extract

Kosher salt and freshly ground black pepper, to taste

1 (10.5-ounce / 298-g) can cream of mushroom soup

1 teaspoon soy sauce

4 cups cooked cut green beans

2 Yukon Gold potatoes, sliced ⅛ inch thick

½ cup heavy cream

½ cup grated Parmesan cheese

1 small garlic clove, finely chopped

1 teaspoon chopped fresh thyme

½ cup mini marshmallows

$^1/_3$ cup crispy fried onions

¼ cup shredded Gruyère cheese

1.   Lightly coat the sheet pans with cooking spray.

2.   Arrange the biscuits down the middle of each sheet pan lengthwise, dividing each pan into two sections.

3.   In a medium bowl, mix together the cranberries, granulated sugar, orange juice, and cornstarch, and set aside.

4.   Put the sweet potatoes in a medium microwave-safe bowl and cover with plastic wrap. Microwave on high for about 12 minutes, or until soft. Add ¼ cup of milk, the butter, brown sugar, and vanilla. Season with salt and pepper. Mash the potatoes with a fork to combine and set aside.

5.   In another medium bowl, combine the cream of mushroom soup, remaining ½ cup of milk, soy sauce, and green beans. Season with salt and pepper. Set aside.

6.   In another medium microwave-safe bowl, place the Yukon Gold potatoes, cream, Parmesan, garlic, and thyme. Season with salt and pepper and stir to combine. Microwave on high for about 6 minutes, or until softened. Set aside.

7.   Pour the cranberry mixture on one side of one of the sheet pans. Spread the sweet potatoes over the other side of the pan and sprinkle them with the marshmallows.

8.   Pour the green bean mixture on one side of the other sheet pan and sprinkle them with the fried onions. Spread the Yukon Gold potato mixture over the other side of the pan and sprinkle with the Gruyère.

9.   Install the wire racks on Levels 1 and 3. Select AIR ROAST, select 2 LEVEL, set the temperature to 350ºF (177ºC), and set the time to 16 minutes. Press START/STOP to begin preheating.

10.   When the unit has preheated, place a sheet pan on each wire rack. Close the oven door to begin cooking.

11.   When cooking is complete, the biscuits will be golden brown. Remove the pans from the oven and let the dishes cool for 5 minutes before serving.

Sweet Potato Casserole with Marshmallows

Prep time: 10 minutes | Cook time: 33 minutes | Serves 8 to 10

3 pounds (1.4 kg) sweet potatoes, peeled and cut into 1-inch cubes

½ cup water

Kosher salt, to taste

1 cup packed light brown sugar

3 tablespoons butter, melted

1½ teaspoons ground cinnamon

1 cup hot milk

2 cups mini marshmallows

½ cup pecans, chopped

1. Divide the sweet potatoes between two large pieces of foil, placing them in the center. Pour the water over the potatoes and season with salt. Wrap the foil around the potatoes, creating two pouches, and seal tightly. Place the foil packets on the sheet pan.

2. Install a wire rack on Level 3. Select BAKE, set the temperature to 400ºF (204ºC), and set the time to 30 minutes. Press START/STOP to begin preheating.

3. When the unit has preheated, place the sheet pan on the wire rack. Close the oven door to begin cooking.

4. When cooking is complete, carefully transfer the potatoes to a large bowl. Add the brown sugar, butter, cinnamon, and milk. Use a fork or potato masher to mash the sweet potatoes to your desired consistency.

5. Transfer the potatoes to the casserole dish. Top them with the marshmallows and pecans.

6. Select BROIL, set the temperature to HI, and set the time to 3 minutes. Press START/STOP to begin.

7. Place the casserole dish on the wire rack and close the oven door to begin cooking.

8. Cooking is done when the marshmallows are golden brown. Remove the dish from the oven and let cool slightly before serving.

Creamy and Cheesy Cauliflower Gratin

Prep time: 15 minutes | Cook time: 35 minutes | Serves 6

1 cup whole milk

1½ cups heavy cream, divided

¼ cup cornstarch

1 (2-pound / 907-g) head cauliflower, cut into 2-inch florets

Kosher salt and freshly ground black pepper, to taste

1 cup plain bread crumbs

1½ cups shredded Parmesan cheese, divided

1.   Pour the milk and 1 cup of cream into a microwave-safe glass bowl. Cover the bowl with plastic wrap, then microwave on high for 3 minutes. Add the cornstarch and whisk well until slightly thickened.

2.   In a large bowl, combine the cauliflower, salt, pepper, bread crumbs, and 1 cup of Parmesan. Pour in the warmed milk and cream, and toss well to mix everything together.

3.   Transfer the mixture to the sheet pan and spread it out so it evenly covers the surface of the pan. Pour the remaining ½ cup of cream evenly over the top.

4.   Install a wire rack on Level 3. Select AIR ROAST, set the temperature to 360ºF (182ºC), and set the time to 35 minutes. Press START/STOP to begin preheating.

5.   When the unit has preheated, place the sheet pan on the wire rack. Close the oven door to begin cooking.

6.   When there are 5 minutes remaining, sprinkle the remaining ½ cup of Parmesan over the top of the cauliflower, then close the oven door to resume cooking.

7.   When cooking is complete, remove the cauliflower gratin from the oven and let cool for at least 5 minutes before serving.

Potato, Carrot, and Parsnip au Gratin

Prep time: 20 minutes | Cook time: 1 hour 10 minutes | Serves 8

3 tablespoons unsalted butter

1 medium onion, diced

2 tablespoons chopped fresh rosemary, divided

2 tablespoons all-purpose flour

3 cups light cream

5 ounces (142 g) Asiago cheese, grated, divided

2 cups shredded Cheddar cheese, divided

2 cups shredded Mozzarella cheese, divided

Kosher salt and freshly ground black pepper, to taste

1 russet potato, peeled and sliced ⅛ inch thick

1 sweet potato, peeled and sliced ⅛ inch thick

3 large carrots, sliced ⅛ inch thick

3 large parsnips, peeled and sliced ⅛ inch thick

¼ cup chopped fresh chives

1. In a small saucepan over medium heat, melt the butter, then add the onion and sauté for about 5 minutes, or until translucent. Add 1 tablespoon of rosemary, then whisk in the flour. Continue whisking until a light brown paste forms (called a roux). Add the cream a little at a time, whisking to dissolve the roux into the cream before adding more.

2. Bring to a boil, then reduce to a simmer and add ½ cup of Asiago, whisking constantly. Then, ½ cup at a time until melted, add 1½ cups of Cheddar and 1½ cups of Mozzarella, whisking constantly to combine, ensuring nothing is stuck to the bottom of the pan. Season with salt and pepper. Remove the pan from the heat.

3. Ladle a little of the sauce on the bottom of the baking dish, swirling to coat it. Layer the russet potato, sweet potato, carrots, and parsnip slices in an overlapping pattern to cover the bottom of the dish. Ladle some cheese sauce over the vegetables, season with salt and pepper, and top with a sprinkling of rosemary. Repeat these layers until all the vegetables, cheese sauce, and rosemary have been used. Cover the dish with foil.

4. Install a wire rack on Level 3. Select AIR ROAST, set the temperature to 360ºF (182ºC), and set the time to 1 hour, 10 minutes. Press START/STOP to begin preheating.

5. When the unit has preheated, place the casserole dish on the wire rack. Close the oven door to begin cooking.

6. When there are 10 minutes remaining, remove the foil and top the vegetables with the remaining grated Asiago, remaining ½ cup of Cheddar, and remaining ½ cup of Mozzarella.

7. Continue cooking for another 8 to 10 minutes, until the cheese on top is golden brown.

8. When cooking is complete, remove the dish from the oven. Let cool slightly, then garnish with the chives and serve.

Parmesan Corn Bread

Prep time: 20 minutes | Cook time: 30 to 35 minutes | Serves 8

Cooking oil spray

1 cup grated Parmesan cheese, divided

4 cups whole milk, divided

½ teaspoon kosher salt

1 cup yellow cornmeal

3 tablespoons unsalted butter

1 cup half-and-half

4 large eggs

1 bunch scallions, white and green parts, chopped

½ cup corn kernels

1.   Coat the casserole dish with cooking spray. Sprinkle the bottom of the dish with 3 tablespoons of Parmesan and set aside.

2.   In a medium saucepan over medium heat, heat 2 cups of milk and the salt until bubbles begin to form around the edges of the pan. Slowly sprinkle in the cornmeal, stirring occasionally.

3.   Reduce the heat to low and cook until the mixture is smooth and creamy. Remove the pan from the heat and add the remaining ¾ cup and 1 tablespoon of Parmesan and the butter. Stir until well incorporated and the butter is melted. Let cool for 10 minutes.

4.   After 10 minutes, combine the cornmeal mixture, the remaining 2 cups of milk, the half-and-half, and eggs in a blender. Blend for about 30 seconds, or until mixed and smooth. Add the scallions and corn, pulse a few times, and pour the mixture into the prepared casserole dish.

5.   Install a wire rack on Level 2. Select BAKE, set the temperature to 350ºF (177ºC), and set the time to 30 minutes. Press START/STOP to begin preheating.

6.   When the unit has preheated, place the casserole dish on the wire rack. Close the oven door to begin cooking.

7.   When the cooking is complete, the spoon bread should be puffy and golden on top. If necessary, cook for up to 5 minutes longer. Serve immediately.

Apple Pies

Prep time: 45 minutes | Cook time: 45 minutes | Serves 16

Cooking oil spray

All-purpose flour, for dusting, plus 4 teaspoons

5 refrigerated rolled piecrusts

5 pounds (2.3 kg) apples, peeled, cored, and sliced ¼ inch thick

½ cup granulated sugar

4 teaspoons flour

2 tablespoons freshly squeezed lemon juice

1 cup (2 sticks) unsalted butter, melted, divided

1 tablespoon ground cinnamon

Kosher salt, to taste

1 cup packed light brown sugar

1 cup light corn syrup

2 teaspoons vanilla extract

5 large eggs, divided, 1 lightly beaten

1½ cups pecan halves, toasted

¼ cup turbinado sugar

1.   Lightly coat the sheet pans with cooking spray.

2.   Lightly flour a clean work surface. Unroll 2 piecrusts and stack them on top of each other. Dust a rolling pin with flour and roll out the layered dough into a large rectangle. Place the dough on one of the sheet pans and gently press the crust into the pan so it comes up the sides and hangs over slightly. Repeat with 2 more pie-crusts. Place both sheet pans in the refrigerator to chill until ready to use.

3.   In a large bowl, combine the apples, granulated sugar, flour, lemon juice, ½ cup of melted butter, cinnamon, and a pinch of salt. Set aside.

4.   In another large bowl, whisk together the brown sugar, corn syrup, remaining ½ cup of melted butter, vanilla, 4 eggs, and a pinch of salt until smooth. Fold in the pecans and set aside.

5.   Remove both baking sheets from the refrigerator. Prick the crusts all over with a fork.

6.   Fill one crust with the pecan filling and the other with the apple filling.

7.   Unroll the remaining piecrust on a lightly floured work surface and roll it out into a large rectangle the size of a sheet pan. Place it on top of the apple filling.

8.   Crimp the edges of both pies and brush the edges and top crust of the apple pie with the beaten egg. Sprinkle the apple pie crust with the turbinado sugar and cut decorative slits in the top crust.

9.   Install the wire racks on Levels 1 and 3. Select BAKE, select 2 LEVEL, set the temperature to 350ºF (177ºC), and set the time to 45 minutes. Press START/STOP to begin preheating.

10.   When the unit has preheated, place the sheet pans on the wire racks. Close the oven door to begin cooking.

11.   Cooking is complete when both pies are set and the crust on the apple pie is golden brown. Let cool slightly before serving.

CHAPTER 9: DESSERTS

Pecan Cookies

Prep time: 25 minutes | Cook time: 10 minutes | Makes 20 cookies

1½ cups pecan halves

1$^1/_3$ cups granulated sugar, divided

$^1/_3$ cup packed dark brown sugar

12 tablespoons (1½ sticks) unsalted butter, at room temperature

1¾ teaspoons kosher salt, divided

½ teaspoon baking soda

1 tablespoon vanilla extract

1 large egg

2 cups all-purpose flour

1½ cups toffee bits or butterscotch chips

1.   Spread the pecans in a single layer on the sheet pan.

2.   Install a wire rack on Level 2. Select BAKE, set the temperature to 350ºF (177ºC), and set the time to 6 minutes. Press START/STOP to begin preheating.

3.   When the unit has preheated, place the sheet pan on the wire rack. Close the oven door to begin cooking.

4.   When cooking is complete, remove the pan from the oven. Let the pecans cool, then chop them.

5.   In a large bowl, combine 1 cup of granulated sugar, the brown sugar, butter, ½ teaspoon of salt, the baking soda, and vanilla. Using a hand mixer or stand mixer, beat until smooth and creamy.

6.   Add the egg and continue to beat until creamy and well incorporated. Scrape down the sides of the bowl with a spatula. Add the flour, toffee bits, and pecans. Mix until fully incorporated.

7.   In a small bowl, combine the remaining $^1/_3$ cup of granulated sugar and 1¼ teaspoons of salt.

8.   Using a spoon, scoop 1- to 1½-inch dough balls. Roll each in the sugar-and-salt mixture, then place them on the sheet pans about 1 inch apart (about 12 cookies per pan). Gently press down on each dough ball to form 2-inch rounds.

9.   Install the wire racks on Levels 1 and 3. Select BAKE, select 2 LEVEL, set the temperature to 350ºF (177ºC), and set the time to 10 minutes. Press START/STOP to begin preheating.

10.   When the unit has preheated, place a sheet pan on each wire rack. Close the oven door to begin cooking.

11.   Cooking is complete when the cookies are crisp and brown at the edges and soft in the center. Carefully remove the sheet pans and place on trivets for the cookies to cool before serving.

Walnut Biscotti with Chocolate Chips

Prep time: 10 minutes | Cook time: 45 minutes | Makes 16 biscotti

1 cup sugar

8 tablespoons (1 stick) unsalted butter or margarine, at room temperature

1 teaspoon vanilla extract

2 large eggs

2½ cups all-purpose flour

3 tablespoons unsweetened cocoa powder

1 tablespoon baking powder

1 teaspoon kosher salt

1 cup mini semisweet chocolate chips

½ cup chopped walnuts

1. In large bowl, beat the sugar and butter with a hand mixer on medium speed, or mix with a spoon. Beat in the vanilla and eggs until smooth. Stir in the flour, cocoa powder, baking powder, and salt. Stir in the chocolate chips and walnuts.

2. Divide the dough between the sheet pans. Shape each dough half into a 10-by-3-inch rectangle.

3. Place the wire racks on Levels 1 and 3. Select BAKE, select 2 LEVEL, set the temperature to 325ºF (163ºC), and set the time to 45 minutes. Press START/STOP to begin preheating.

4. When the unit has preheated, place a sheet pan on each wire rack. Close the oven door to begin cooking.

5. When there are 20 minutes remaining, check to see that a toothpick inserted in the center of each rectangle comes out clean. Press START/STOP to pause cooking. Remove the sheet pans from the oven and let cool for 10 minutes.

6. Transfer the rectangles to a cutting board, and using a sharp knife, cut each crosswise into 8 equal slices. Place the slices cut-side down on the sheet pans. Place the sheet pans back on the wire racks and close the oven door. Press START/STOP to continue cooking.

7. Bake for about 10 minutes, or until golden brown and dry on top. Turn over the biscotti and bake for about 10 minutes longer, or until golden brown and dry. Remove the sheet pans from the oven and place on wire racks to cool.

Chocolate and Macadamia Cookie Bars

Prep time: 15 minutes | Cook time: 20 minutes | Makes 24 bars

1 cup (2 sticks) unsalted butter, at room temperature

1 cup firmly packed light brown sugar

1 cup granulated sugar

3 large eggs

1½ teaspoons vanilla extract

¾ teaspoon baking soda

¾ teaspoon kosher salt

3 cups all-purpose flour

1 cup chocolate chips

1 cup white chocolate chips

1 cup crushed salted macadamia nuts

1. Using a hand mixer or stand mixer, beat the butter, brown sugar, and granulated sugar until smooth. Add the eggs and vanilla and mix until well combined.
2. In a large bowl, stir the baking soda and salt into the flour. Slowly add the flour to the wet ingredients, mixing until just combined.
3. Transfer half of the dough to another large bowl. Fold the chocolate chips into the dough in one bowl and the white chocolate chips and macadamia nuts into the dough in the other bowl.
4. Line the sheet pan with parchment paper. Spread the chocolate chip cookie dough onto half of the sheet pan. Spread the white chocolate and macadamia dough on the other half of the pan. Use a spatula or your fingers to spread out each evenly.
5. Install a wire rack on Level 3. Select BAKE, set the temperature to 350ºF (177ºC), and set the time to 20 minutes. Press START/STOP to begin preheating.
6. When the unit has preheated, place the sheet pan on the wire rack. Close the oven door to begin cooking.
7. When cooking is complete, remove the sheet pan from the oven and place on a wire rack to cool. Cut into 24 bars.

Strawberry Crumble Bars

Prep time: 15 minutes | Cook time: 30 minutes | Makes 16 bars

1½ cups (3 sticks) unsalted butter, at room temperature

1½ cups packed light brown sugar

½ cup granulated sugar

2¾ cups old-fashioned rolled oats

2 cups all-purpose flour

1 teaspoon vanilla extract

1 teaspoon kosher salt

1 teaspoon baking powder

1 (18-ounce / 510-g) jar strawberry jam

½ cup peanut butter

1. Using a hand mixer or stand mixer, beat together the butter, brown sugar, and granulated sugar until smooth.

2. Add the oats, flour, vanilla, salt, and baking powder and stir until thoroughly combined.

3. Transfer two-thirds of the crumb mixture to the sheet pan and press it into an even, flat layer (it should go about three-quarters of the way up the side of the pan).

4. Spread the jam evenly over the crust, leaving a ½-inch border along the edges. Use a ½-tablespoon measuring spoon to dollop the peanut butter evenly on top of the jam.

5. Sprinkle the remaining crumb mixture over the top.

6. Install a wire rack on Level 3. Select BAKE, set the temperature to 350ºF (177ºC), and set the time to 30 minutes. Press START/STOP to begin preheating.

7. When the unit has preheated, place the sheet pan on the wire rack. Close the oven door to begin cooking.

8. When cooking is complete, remove the pan from the oven and let cool completely before cutting into squares.

Lime Pie Bars

Prep time: 15 minutes | Cook time: 22 minutes | Makes 16 bars

8 tablespoons (1 stick) unsalted butter, melted

3 cups graham cracker crumbs

½ cup sugar

2 (14-ounce / 397-g) cans sweetened condensed milk

2 large eggs

2 tablespoons grated lime zest

1¼ cups freshly squeezed or bottled key lime juice

½ teaspoon kosher salt

Whipped cream (optional)

1.   Line the sheet pan with parchment paper. Make a diagonal cut in each corner of parchment so it can lay flat. Set aside.

2.   In a large bowl, mix together the melted butter, graham cracker crumbs, and sugar.

3.   Pour the crumb mixture onto the prepared sheet pan, and use the bottom of a glass to press the crust into an even, flat layer.

4.   Install a wire rack on Level 3. Select BAKE, set the temperature to 350ºF (177ºC), and set the time to 22 minutes. Press START/STOP to begin preheating.

5.   When the unit has preheated, place the sheet pan on the wire rack. Close the oven door to begin cooking.

6.   Meanwhile, in a medium bowl, whisk together the sweetened condensed milk, eggs, lime zest, lime juice, and salt. Set aside.

7.   When there are 12 minutes remaining, remove the sheet pan from the oven and pour the filling over the crust, using a spatula to spread it into an even layer. Place the sheet pan back on the wire rack and close the oven door to continue cooking.

8.   When cooking is complete, remove the pan from the oven and let cool completely. Once cooled, place the sheet pan in the refrigerator to chill for at least 1 hour.

9.   Once chilled, cut into squares and serve with whipped cream (if using).

Chocolate Fudgy Brownies

Prep time: 30 minutes | Cook time: 45 minutes | Serves 12

For the Brownie Layer:

4 ounces (113 g) unsweetened baking chocolate, broken into small pieces

1 cup (2 sticks) unsalted butter, at room temperature, plus more for greasing

4 large eggs

2 cups granulated sugar

1 cup all-purpose flour

1 tablespoon vanilla extract

For the Topping:

4 ounces (113 g) unsweetened baking chocolate, broken into small pieces

1 cup (2 sticks) unsalted butter, at room temperature

4 cups powdered sugar

2 large eggs

1 tablespoon vanilla extract

3 to 4 cups mini marshmallows

1. To make the brownie layer: Put the chocolate and butter in an oven-safe bowl.
2. Install a wire rack on Level 3. Select BAKE, set the temperature to 350ºF (177ºC), and set the time to 5 minutes. Press START/STOP to begin preheating.
3. When unit has preheated, place the bowl on the wire rack. Close the oven door to begin cooking.
4. Meanwhile, in a large bowl, use a hand mixer or stand mixer to combine the eggs, granulated sugar, flour, and vanilla.
5. When cooking is complete, remove the bowl from the oven and stir the chocolate and butter until well combined. Pour the chocolate mixture into the batter and mix to combine.
6. Grease the baking pan with butter (or cooking spray). Pour the brownie batter into the pan and spread it into an even layer.
7. Select BAKE, set the temperature to 350ºF (177ºC), and set the time to 35 minutes. Press START/STOP to begin preheating.
8. When the unit has preheated, place the sheet pan on the wire rack. Close the oven door to begin cooking.
9. When cooking is complete, remove the pan from the oven and let cool completely.
10. To make the topping: Put the chocolate and butter in an oven-safe bowl.
11. Leave the wire rack on Level 3. Select BAKE, set the temperature to 350ºF (177ºC), and set the time to 5 minutes. Press START/STOP to begin preheating.
12. When unit has preheated, place the bowl on the wire rack. Close the oven door to begin cooking.
13. When cooking is complete, remove the bowl from the oven and stir the chocolate and butter until well combined.
14. Pour the chocolate mixture into a large bowl and add the powdered sugar, eggs, and vanilla. Mix until well combined. Stir in the marshmallows.
15. Spread the topping onto the cooled brownies. Chill in the refrigerator for at least 1 hour before cutting.

Pretzel and Hazelnut Brownies

Prep time: 20 minutes | Cook time: 35 minutes | Serves 10 to 15

1 cup (2 sticks) unsalted butter, at room temperature, plus more for greasing

1½ cups sugar

1 teaspoon vanilla extract

4 large eggs

½ cup hazelnut spread, plus more for topping

1¾ cups all-purpose flour

½ cup unsweetened cocoa powder

½ teaspoon kosher salt

1 cup mini pretzels, crushed into small pieces, plus more for topping

1. Grease the baking pans with butter and set aside.

2. In a stand mixer with the paddle attachment, beat the butter, sugar, and vanilla on medium speed until smooth. Reduce the mixer speed to low. Add the eggs one at a time, incorporating each completely before adding the next egg. Add the hazelnut spread and mix on low speed for 30 seconds, or until fully incorporated.

3. Turn the mixer off and use a spatula to scrape down the sides of the bowl. Add the flour, cocoa powder, and salt, and mix on low speed until well combined. Using a spatula, stir in the crushed pretzels. Divide the batter evenly between the two baking pans.

4. Install the wire racks on Levels 1 and 3. Select BAKE, select 2 LEVEL, set the temperature to 350ºF (177ºC), and set the time to 35 minutes. Press START/STOP to begin preheating.

5. When the unit has preheated, place a baking pan on each wire rack. Close the oven door to begin cooking.

6. Cooking is complete when a toothpick inserted in the center of the brownies comes out clean. Remove the pans from the oven and let cool completely. Spread a thin layer of hazelnut spread on top of the brownies and sprinkle with additional crushed pretzel pieces.

Ritzy Candy Bar and Cookie Cake

Prep time: 10 minutes | Cook time: 45 minutes | Serves 10

Cooking oil spray

3 (16-ounce / 454-g) packages prepared chocolate chip cookie dough

2 (2-ounce / 57-g) Snickers bars, cut into 1-inch pieces

2 (2-ounce / 57-g) 3 Musketeers bars, cut into 1-inch pieces

2 (2-ounce / 57-g) Peppermint Patties, cut into 2-inch pieces

2 (2-ounce / 57-g) packages Peanut M&M's

1 (15-ounce / 425-g) jar vanilla frosting

1.   Cut a piece of parchment paper or foil into a circle that is approximately the same diameter as the bottom of the cake pan. Place the parchment paper or foil in the bottom of the pan. Cut a long strip of parchment paper or foil and wrap it along the inside wall of the pan. Use a light spray of oil as "glue" to keep the parchment paper or foil against the wall of the pan.

2.   Place 1 package of cookie dough in the bottom of the pan. Press the dough so that it covers the bottom in an even layer.

3.   Cover the dough with half of the Snickers bars, half of the 3 Musketeers bars, half of the Peppermint Patties, and half of the Peanut M&M's in an even layer.

4.   Repeat the layers with the second package of cookie dough and the remaining candy.

5.   Press the third package of cookie dough on top to form the cake.

6.   Install a wire rack on Level 3. Select BAKE, set the temperature to 350ºF (177ºC), and set the time to 45 minutes. Press START/STOP to begin preheating.

7.   When the unit has preheated, place the sheet pan on the wire rack. Close the oven door to begin cooking.

8.   When cooking is complete, let the cake cool in the refrigerator for at least 2 hours.

9.   Release the springform pan and invert the cake onto a cutting board or cake plate to remove. Turn the cake right-side up and spread the frosting evenly over the top and sides of the cake. Cut and serve.

Blackberry and Raspberry Hand Pies

Prep time: 15 minutes | Cook time: 25 minutes | Serves 6

1 (7.5-ounce / 213-g) roll store-bought pie dough

½ cup frozen blackberries

½ cup frozen raspberries

1 teaspoon freshly squeezed lemon juice

1 teaspoon vanilla extract

3 tablespoons granulated sugar, plus 2 teaspoons

1 tablespoon cornstarch

¼ teaspoon ground cinnamon

2 tablespoons whole milk

1.   Unroll the pie dough and use a 4½-inch round biscuit cutter to cut 4 circles of dough, then reroll the scrap dough to the same thickness and cut out 2 more circles of dough.

2.   In a small bowl, combine the blackberries and raspberries with the lemon juice and vanilla, and toss to coat the berries. This will help the sugar mixture stick.

3.   In another small bowl, mix 3 tablespoons of sugar, the cornstarch, and cinnamon until there are no clumps. Add the mixture to the bowl with the berries, and toss to coat.

4.   Line the sheet pan with parchment paper. Place the circles of pie dough on the pan and brush each with the milk. Divide the filling evenly among the dough circles.

5.   Fold the pie dough over the filling and seal the edges with your fingers. Crimp the edges with a fork.

6.   Using a paring knife, poke a hole in the top of each pie. Brush the tops with milk and sprinkle with the remaining 2 teaspoons of sugar.

7.   Install a wire rack on Level 3. Select BAKE, set the temperature to 350ºF (177ºC), and set the time to 25 minutes. Press START/STOP to begin preheating.

8.   When the unit has preheated, place the sheet pan on the wire rack. Close the oven door to begin cooking.

9.   Halfway through cooking, open the door and rotate the sheet pan. Close the oven door to continue cooking.

10.   When cooking is complete, remove the pan from the oven and let the hand pies cool.

Pumpkin and Crusty Bread Pudding

Prep time: 15 minutes | Cook time: 30 minutes | Serves 6 to 8

1 cup pumpkin purée (not pumpkin pie filling)

1 cup packed dark brown sugar

3 large eggs

1 cup whole milk

½ cup heavy cream

½ cup cold brew coffee or espresso

1 tablespoon vanilla extract

2 teaspoons pumpkin pie spice

4 cups cubed day-old crusty bread, preferably French bread (but any kind works)

8 tablespoons (1 stick) unsalted butter, melted

Cooking oil spray

1.   Mix together the pumpkin purée, brown sugar, eggs, milk, cream, coffee, vanilla, and pumpkin pie spice.

2.   In a large bowl, toss the bread with the butter. Pour over the pumpkin mixture and fold until the bread is coated.

3.   Lightly coat the casserole dish with cooking spray. Pour the bread mixture into the dish.

4.   Install a wire rack on Level 3. Select BAKE, set the temperature to 350ºF (177ºC), and set the time to 30 minutes. Press START/STOP to begin preheating.

5.   When the unit has preheated, place the casserole dish on the wire rack. Close the oven door to begin cooking.

6.   When cooking is complete, the top of the bread pudding will be golden brown. Remove the dish from the oven and let cool slightly before serving.